Charting a Course for Conscious Business

HOLISTIC IMPACT
The Ubuntu Polder Journey

Bruno Olierhoek

Holistic Impact

Copyright © 2024 by Bruno Olierhoek

All rights reserved

Published by Red Penguin Books

Bellerose Village, New York

Library of Congress Control Number: 2024912839

ISBN

Print 978-1-63777-588-2

Digital 978-1-63777-587-5

PRAISE FOR BRUNO OLIERHOEK

"Unleashing Conscious Leadership" is a captivating exploration of ethical leadership through the eyes of Bruno Olierhoek. This inspiring narrative reveals the transformative power of integrating purpose and responsibility in business. A must-read for future leaders committed to making a positive impact on the world."

Martin Lindstrom, *New York Times* best-selling author of *Buyology* and *Ministry of Common Sense*

"Bruno's relentless dedication to holistic impact resonates deeply with my own commitment to circularity. Having collaborated on projects that brought the Ubuntu Polder Framework to life, I can attest to the transformative power of his approach. A must-read for all doers striving to make a meaningful difference in the world."

Professor Gunter Pauli, entrepreneur, economist and author of numerous books, including the seminal work *The Blue Economy; 10 Years, 100 Innovations, 100 Million Jobs*

"Bruno challenges us to lead with purpose, break free from conventional boundaries, and show courage in our complex and fast-moving world."

Paul Polman, business leader, campaigner, and co-author of *Net Positive: How Courageous Companies Thrive by Giving More Than They Take*

"Having witnessed Bruno in action, I can attest to the transformative impact of his approach outlined in Holistic Impact: The Ubuntu Polder Framework Journey. This book offers invaluable insights derived from real-world experiences, guiding leaders to navigate the complexities of business with purpose and drive."

Nandu Nandkishore, former Global CEO Nestlé Nutrition, Mentor Capitalist, Adjunct Professor at the Indian School of Business, co-author of *The Dance of Disruption and Creation: Epochal Change* and the *Opportunity for Enterprise*

FOREWORD

Writing a book introduction is a balancing act between engaging the reader and not revealing too much of the plot. I had the privilege of being one of the first readers, and I want to share my initial reflection. Holistic Impact is a fascinating personal journey of self-discovery, where Bruno reflects on his career as a business executive. My initial reaction, after reading only a few chapters, was that this book is the ESG version of Zen and the art of motorcycle maintenance. Different content, similar journey.

In his book, *Holistic Impact*, Bruno shares his personal journey, life experience and the philosophy he has developed. There are two pillars: Ubuntu – benefiting a community and eco-system rather than narrow self-interest; and Polder – finding pragmatic solutions rather than overthinking. But I leave it to the reader to discover the details.

A bit of context. I first met Bruno in 2008 when he attended the Program for Executive Development at IMD Business School. Being sponsored by Nestlé for this ten-week program was a clear indication of his high potential within the company. In the program, Bruno stood out in many ways, but the perhaps most notable achievement was being selected the most valuable participant by his fellow students in both two modules.

After the program, Bruno embarked on a career spanning some of the most challenging frontier markets in Africa and Asia. Independently, I developed a strong interest in business development in Africa, especially related to the challenge of serving the bottom of the pyramid (very poor consumers). We reunited when Bruno became CEO & Chairman of Nestlé's South and East African region, first in Zimbabwe and later in Kenya, with many collaborations and enlightening discussions as a result.

Doing business as for the greater good in emerging countries requires creativity, local knowhow, and the ability to find unorthodox but pragmatic solutions to complex challenges. Even more, it requires demonstrating authentic leadership in implementing them. Bruno manifests all of them, starting with a genuine interest in exploring and connecting with the essence of each country. One example is his passion for photography, which has enriched his ability to propose a unique and inclusive leadership style. This approach was recognized in winning the Conscious Companies Award.

Holistic Impact provides an innovative and important perspective on doing business for a higher cause and is a very enjoyable read.

Leif Sjöblom

Professor of Financial Management

IMD Business School, Switzerland

CONTENTS

ONE

INTRODUCTION: UNLEASHING CONSCIOUS LEADERSHIP.

SETTING THE STAGE FOR TRANSFORMATION

n the vibrant landscape of business and leadership, there exists an innovative initiative that seeks to unveil the torch-bearers of conscious, ethical leadership and their organizations. It is the annual Conscious Companies Award in South Africa – a cherished accolade that honors and reveres visionary leaders. These leaders grasp the profound significance of conscious leadership as a way of life, both in the realm of business and in the broader world. They are individuals whose very essence, purpose, humanity, and sense of responsibility ripple through their organizations, creating a transformative impact.

I vividly recall the moment when Saint Francis, our Head of Corporate Affairs, walked into my office with a surprising announcement: I had been nominated for the Conscious Companies Leadership Award. It was an unexpected turn of events, yet it struck a resonant chord deep within me. The topic of conscious leadership was close to my heart, and the esteemed jury, led by the venerable Judge Professor Mervyn E. King, added to the intrigue. As I greenlit the process, the journey began with a deluge of documentation about our company and its evolution over the years. It was followed by candid phone interviews and on-camera discussions. No scripted answers, just my unfiltered perspective on leadership and company stewardship.

Several months into this transformative odyssey, I received an invitation to the Conscious Companies 2021 Awards night. Seated at table number one, in the heart of Melrose Arch, Rosebank, South Africa, I was surrounded by fascinating individuals. The evening unfolded, a tapestry of inspiring stories, revealing leaders who had left an indelible mark not only within their organizations but in the communities and societies they touched – leaders who were consciously humanizing business.

And then, the moment of truth arrived: "And the winner is... Bruno Olierhoek, please come to the stage."

It was a proud moment, not just for me but for my entire team, many of whom were watching the event online. The bright lights shone on us, but what was most illuminating was the sight of fellow South African leaders rising to their feet, applauding the message of conscious leadership. It was a moment that required time to fully absorb.

Days later, as I reflected on this achievement, I realized that while consciousness and conscious leadership are terms widely acknowledged, few of us have delved deeply into their profound implications. So, I had won, and with it, a place on the Conscious Companies Council. A genuine honor. I was now poised to contribute to the noble cause of spreading consciousness in the world. To do so, I needed answers to fundamental questions: What is consciousness? What is my role in it? How conscious a leader have I been, and how can I further my journey as a conscious leader? These questions percolated within me, leading to an influx of queries: Why isn't consciousness better understood? Why isn't it a more prominent subject in the business world? Why does it sometimes seem fluffy when, in reality, it is not?

As the newest member of the Conscious Companies Council, I was invited to speak at the Annual Conscious Leadership Summit in 2022. This opportunity compelled me to crystallize my thoughts on conscious leadership in a concise format. My allotted ten minutes became a springboard for profound discussions, igniting the spark that would eventually lead to this book.

In the process of writing, I discovered that my drive and motivation have always transcended the boundaries of organizational objectives. I've harnessed the company's resources to serve a personal purpose that aligns with the greater purpose of the organization. I am intrinsically motivated to make a positive impact not only for the company but also for the world at large. This intrinsic motivation mirrors the spirit I observe in today's youth, the next generation of leaders. They hunger for knowledge, and they are committed to taking action to shape the world. This book is primarily for these forward-thinking leaders.

For me, doing business and my career as an international expatriate have always been a means to an end, a journey to explore the world's diversity. Every country, each with its unique stars, landscapes, wildlife, food, culture, and perspectives, has allowed me to continually question my identity and the world. It has inspired me to "taste the world," to immerse myself fully, to experience and live consciously, to be present in the now, to be kind, and to do good. Working as an expat in a multinational with a noble purpose perfectly aligned with this aspiration. Over the years, I've strived to seize every opportunity to embrace life and make the most of the sights and experiences.

I've always been an active and entrepreneurial individual, both in my professional and personal life. My driving force has been to explore the world actively, to make things happen, and to contribute positively to society's challenges. This has led me to initiatives that hold meaningful impacts and the potential for global scalability. As an international executive, I've been privileged to work across diverse markets in Asia, Europe, and

Africa. I've served as the Chairman and CEO of Nestlé for the East and Southern Africa Region (ESAR) and as the CEO of Nestlé Pakistan. My journey in Pakistan included the role of President of the Overseas Investors Chamber of Commerce & Industry, representing 191 international companies from 35 countries. Throughout my career, I've been immersed in the multifaceted world of business and leadership, consistently pursuing lasting change.

In my quest to drive holistic impact, I've delved into unique business models and initiatives, aiming to benefit not just the company but also communities and the planet. Initiatives such as RE2AL (Realizing Empowered and Enabled African Livelihoods), ZiWeb (Zimbabwe Women Empowered in Business), and using spent coffee grounds to grow oyster mushrooms are examples that showcase how business can be a force for good. These initiatives garnered recognition and media attention, but they were products of a long and transformative journey – a journey I'm eager to share. It has led me to a way of doing business that results in a real win-win-win scenario: a win for the business, a win for communities, and a win for the planet.

Doubt and uncertainty are constants in life, and I've had my share. These moments of hesitation can be especially profound during one's teenage years. Currently, I have three teenagers of my own, and I've consistently encouraged them to embrace these moments. Early in my life, I adopted the habit of uprooting myself and my family every three to five years, moving across continents from Europe to South-East Asia, back to Europe, to Central Africa, to South Asia, to Southern and East Africa and finally to our current base in the UAE in the Middle-East. These experiences have been a blessing, shaping not only my family's understanding but also revealing patterns in life. They have empowered me to create a model for holistic impact, generating value for shareholders, creating jobs, uplifting communities, and restoring nature simultaneously.

4

The thought often arises: Is there anything truly new under the sun? For years, I wrestled with the notion of original thinking and hesitated to write a book. Then, I came across a powerful idea – that all art is theft, as articulated by Pablo Picasso. This notion liberated me to share my thoughts and perspectives more freely. In this book, I aim to reflect on my past, distill my learnings, shed light on the world's challenges, and engage in conversations about the future while remaining grounded in the present.

In a recent interview, I was asked, "What is the one thing you wish somebody had told you when you were starting out?" My response was simple: "You have to learn to trust the Universe."

A conversation with Brenda Kali, the CEO of Conscious Company, further nudged me toward writing this book. It's a challenging endeavor, but I've decided to heed my own advice and trust the Universe. As Kierkegaard wisely noted, "to dare is to risk one's footing, to not dare is to risk losing oneself."

I've always had two projects on my "to do list" that I kept procrastinating: writing a book and creating a website for my photography. Over the years, I've accumulated a treasure trove of photographs, capturing the rich tapestry of the world. While writing sometimes feels like rambling, photographs have a unique power to tell a story that leaves ample room for interpretation. They are, in essence, a form of high-context language. Books, on the other hand, tend to present the author's perspective in a low-context manner. I've always found greater resonance in the freedom that images offer, unburdened by the judgments that can sometimes accompany words.

My unwavering curiosity, my hunger for learning, and my natural inclination for exploration have guided me to where I stand today. The Universe has orchestrated my journey, placing me precisely where I need to be.

My life's path has been instrumental in shaping me. While the world grapples with myriad challenges, I remain grateful for the opportunity to explore, experience, and become a part of it. The experiences have formed an internal compass that informs my choices, no matter how messy life may be. It's not a dogmatic statement of purpose but a feeling that serves as my guiding star. More than ever, I've started to listen to my body, to trust my instincts and gut, as much as I do my intellect and mind.

Before we dive deeper, I want to acknowledge that as I penned this book and looked back on my life, I may occasionally sound as if I had always been clear about my path. However, there's a fascinating concept called the illusion of continuity, which posits that we don't truly know what our future selves desire. Embracing this dilemma, I endorse three pieces of advice: Be Curious, Stay Humble in your communication, and Be Courageous in your pursuits. They have the power to shape your future self and help you adapt as you grow older and gain more life experiences.

After almost three decades in the corporate world, I continue to believe in the power of business as a force for good. However, not all leadership teams and CEOs know where or how to start becoming a more conscious company. I therefore decided, after my experiences as an international expat across different continents, it was time to channel my energy and passion into setting up my consultancy and advisory company in Dubai, named Ubuntu. My mission was clear: to assist leadership teams and CEOs embark on a holistic business transformation journey, embedding digital, sustainability, circularity, and ESG principles at the heart of their business models. I believe that my experience and life journey as captured in this book can be a catalyst for change creating a WIN-WIN-WIN for companies, communities, and the planet.

TWO
THE URGENCY OF CHANGE: NAVIGATING SUSTAINABLE TRANSFORMATION

CRITICAL OBSERVATIONS AND WAKE-UP CALLS

In a world teetering on the brink of transformation, where the winds of progress and the turbulence of crisis converge, the case for change stands as the rallying cry of our time. The old paradigms are crumbling, their foundations weakened by the relentless march of time and the echoes of a planet yearning for renewal. We find ourselves at the crossroads of history, where the choices we make will ripple through generations, reshaping not only our businesses but the very essence of our world.

In the cocoon of complacency, where the echoes of outdated dogmas and unsustainable practices still resonate, we confront a stark truth: the "business as usual" model, rooted in the exploitation of finite resources for infinite growth (and ever increasing profit margin expectations), is an ideology of the past. It's a model that, in its pursuit of profit above all else, has sown the seeds of environmental degradation, social inequity, and moral decay. The time has come to transcend this antiquated blueprint and embrace a new vision—a vision rooted in the profound interconnectedness of our world, a vision that acknowledges the symbiotic relationship between businesses and society, and a vision that reveres the ecosystems upon which our very survival depends.

This is the call to arms, the clarion call for change—the clarion call for Ubuntu, for a new paradigm that I call "the Ubuntu Polder Framework." Ubuntu, a Southern African philosophy that transcends the boundaries of creed and color, teaches us that "I am because we are." It underscores the inescapable truth that our destinies are interwoven, our fates entangled in the intricate web of existence. The Ubuntu Polder Framework is a guide, a blueprint for the future—a model that implores us to cooperate, to nurture our collective understanding of the world's interconnectedness, and to create value for all stakeholders, while simultaneously igniting the flames of employment and the restoration of nature.

The heart of this model lies in the belief that businesses must become the solution to societal needs, their rewards intrinsically tied to their contributions. It's a departure from the old paradigm where profit overshadowed purpose, where success often came at the expense of the world's well-being. The Ubuntu Polder Framework ushers in a new era of business—a golden age of conscientious leadership and a commitment to leave no one behind.

But this isn't merely a lofty ideal; it's a paradigm I've lived and breathed. For 27 years, I navigated the intricate world of corporate life, straddling continents and cultures, seeking to implement this model myself. Holistic business transformation is not an abstract theory—it's a reality I've witnessed, a journey I've undertaken, and an ethos I've seen yield remarkable results. From upstream endeavors to mid-stream initiatives and downstream projects, the Ubuntu Polder Framework has shown its versatility and adaptability, demonstrating that it can transcend industries, sectors, and borders.

This book is not just a narrative—it's a manifesto for change, a testament to the belief that business is a force for good. Together, we will explore the core principles of the Ubuntu Polder Framework and its application in diverse contexts. We will delve into real-world examples and profound insights, uncovering the mechanisms by which businesses can serve as catalysts for transformation.

The journey ahead is bold, ambitious, and, above all, indispensable. The time for change is now, and this is our clarion call. As we embark on this voyage of discovery, let us remember the words of Margaret Mead: "Never doubt that a small group of thoughtful, committed citizens can change the world; indeed, it's the only thing that ever has." We are those citizens, and change is our calling. Let us take the first step towards the future we envision, a future where business harmonizes with society, a future where Ubuntu reigns supreme.

Witnessing the Issues Firsthand

In the crucible of my international experiences, I've been an eyewitness to the pressing issues that transcend borders. This section chronicles the firsthand encounters with the challenges that demand our attention—social inequalities, environmental degradation, and the unsustainable pursuit of growth. It's a visceral exploration of the realities that fuel the urgency for transformative action.

For some, the ordinary is extraordinary; for others, it's exotic. My journey, often captured through the lens of my phone as a basic camera, is one that transcends boundaries and defies expectations. It's a journey rooted in the belief that change begins with perception, that the world is not as narrow as we might think.

As I embarked on my life as an international expatriate, I was met with a barrage of well-intentioned but naive warnings each time I set foot in a new country. "Don't go to Indonesia, it's over-crowded and prone to violence," they said. "Avoid Vietnam; the shadow of Agent Orange lingers, and the land is yet to be fully de-mined." "The Philippines is fraught with coup d'états and kidnappings." "Cameroon, the heart of Africa, teems with diseases and misery." "Pakistan is infested with terrorists," they cautioned. "South Africa is a hotbed of crime."

These warnings reflected a distorted world view, shaped by the media and perpetuated by the limited experiences of many. The brain, always eager to conserve energy, often resorts to simplistic stereotypes. It's a phenomenon that became apparent to me during my university days when I was involved in the UN's 50th anniversary celebrations.

Representing my university, I joined students from across Europe in Geneva for a week of UN agency visits and discussions about the future. As the week concluded, we were gathered in the general assembly hall and asked, "What is your pledge to make the world a better place?" Many offered grand promises to end hunger or abolish slavery, noble ambitions to be sure. But I couldn't help but ponder the concrete actions that would bring about these lofty goals. When it was my turn, I pledged to work in the developing world, striving to make a tangible impact through kindness in my household, community, and the sphere of influence my career would provide. That pledge has remained with me, a guiding light in my journey.

My commitment to business was never solely about profit; it was about doing good, about leaving a lasting legacy, and about maximizing my time on this planet. My career with Nestlé, which began at the tender age of 18, led me to traverse the globe, shouldering increasing responsibilities. I transitioned through diverse functions, culminating in personal P&L accountability since 2005. I took on the role of CEO in markets of varying sizes, and in my last four and a half years, I presided over a region spanning 23 countries and 8 factories.

My ethos now revolves around holistic impact—where solid financial results marry with people development, benefiting communities and our planet. Throughout this book, I will unravel the origins of this ethos, its practical applications in my life and work, and the imperative belief that we cannot sit idly, waiting for miraculous solutions to appear. Instead, we must each take practical steps in the right direction.

In my years living across continents, I've been a firsthand witness to the global issues often spoken of abstractly in the media. It is apparent to me that the world needs a profound awakening—a wake-up call to the ticking time bombs we've created. Yet, in the face of these seemingly insurmountable dilemmas, I've also observed that solutions do exist. Within my sphere of influence, I've implemented initiatives that yielded astounding results—results that benefit our communities, our environment, and the very essence of business.

The prevailing ethos of modern business leadership fixates on profits at the perceived expense of communities and the environment. But in my personal journey, I've come to realize that with the right perspective, it's possible to achieve both profit and positive impact. In the pages that follow, we will explore how this paradigm shift is not only attainable but imperative, and how we can embrace a new model of doing business that harmonizes profit with societal well-being.

A Collective Yearning for Change

Amidst the global tapestry of diverse cultures and landscapes, there emerges a collective yearning for change. This section amplifies the voices of individuals and communities around the world who share a common desire for a more sustainable and equitable future. It's a testament to the shared aspirations that bind us together in the quest for meaningful transformation.

Countless conversations with young leaders, a new generation infused with energy and passion, have provided me with a unique window into their fervent desire for change. I've had the privilege of mentoring many of these emerging leaders, whether within the organizations I've worked for or among the visionary entrepreneurs I've collaborated with. Additionally, my role as a guest professor at the IMD Business School allowed me to engage with bright minds eager to reshape the world. Over the course of my 28-year corporate journey and my involvement in the Young Presidents Organization (YPO), where I've connected with CEOs, ambassadors, ministers, and even heads of state, one common thread weaves through all these interactions: the collective realization that the world is at a crossroads, and the clamor for change reverberates in our hearts and minds.

In these diverse encounters, a shared sentiment emerges—a recognition of the profound issues confronting our planet and an earnest yearning to be part of the solution. We all stand on the precipice of transformation, united by a desire to reshape the world for the better. Yet, the path forward remains elusive, and frustration often shadows our aspirations.

Studies have illuminated a striking generational difference in mindset—a divergence in beliefs about the feasibility of implementing change and the urgency to drive it. Among the Gen Y and Z cohorts, a remarkable 79% prioritize their career choices based on environmental and ethical principles. This not only influences where they choose to work but also ripples through their purchasing decisions and dietary preferences. The younger generations are, in essence, amplifying their voices through their choices, demanding a world that aligns with their values.

The world we find ourselves in today seems adrift, lacking a clear direction or a unifying leadership. It's a time when we must come together to deliberate on how we move forward and rediscover our collective consciousness.

With each turn of a newspaper page or the flicker of the news on our screens, we are inundated with increasingly alarming facts about the state of our planet. Do you ever find yourself pondering the magnitude of the world's challenges and wonder how you or your company can contribute to the solutions for these pressing global issues?

We're all acutely aware of the palpable uncertainty that defines our times, often encapsulated by the acronym VUCA—Volatility, Uncertainty, Complexity, and Ambiguity. This term, coined back in 1987, paints a vivid picture of the landscape we navigate. But for every problem, there's a solution, and the world now craves a VUCA response: Vision, Understanding, Clarity, and Agility.

Undoubtedly, change is necessary, but let's not overlook the silver linings amidst the challenges. In the book *Factfulness*, Hans Rosling meticulously unravels the world's realities, offering ten compelling reasons why our perceptions often mislead us, and why things are, in fact, better than we tend to believe.

Yet, while people across the globe are enjoying longer, healthier lives, it's undeniable that the world is in the throes of transformation. The locus of global power has shifted from the Atlantic to the Pacific and Indian Oceans, and as migration surges, minorities are emerging as the new majority. This shift, from rural to urban, from the north to the global south, necessitates our ability to embrace diversity. Moreover, we grapple with the challenge of mounting unemployment and an ever-widening wealth gap. In the United States, the top 0.1% possesses as much wealth as the bottom 90%, and in our digitally interconnected world, this disparity is no longer hidden; it's visible to all. These are the seeds of social unrest, a stark reminder that our world is at a crossroads.

Surprisingly, COVID was Not the Wake-Up Call

While the world grappled with the seismic impact of the COVID-19 pandemic, it became evident that the wake-up call for transformation transcended the immediate health crisis. Surprisingly, it wasn't the pandemic alone that shook the foundations; rather, it exposed and exacerbated existing systemic issues. This section untangles the complexities of the post-COVID landscape, revealing why the imperative for change goes beyond the pandemic's immediate wake-up call.

In an unexpected turn of events, the COVID pandemic failed to serve as the profound wake-up call the world urgently requires. The human inclination for equilibrium is a powerful force, and indeed, our current economic model has achieved remarkable feats, lifting countless individuals out of poverty. However, at its core, we find a troubling reality: the unrestrained consumption of finite resources—energy and materials—driving our insatiable hunger for perpetual growth.

This behavior is consistently reinforced as we continue to gauge our success through metrics like Gross Domestic Product (GDP) and stock market performance. But what exactly does success mean? Is an increase in GDP synonymous with an increase of global happiness? Countless studies attest that beyond a certain threshold of income, the pursuit of wealth fails to augment our well-being. Many of us reached this threshold long ago, and yet we persist in complicating our lives with superfluous possessions that offer no genuine satisfaction. The best things in life, as the age-old saying goes, are indeed free, yet the allure of material possessions and status, as well as the worrying that we might not have enough in the future often compels us to amass more, rather than to give, share, and help others. During Covid this was clearly demonstrated through hoarding at individual levels of toilet paper and the hoarding of western countries of COVID vaccines.

Though the COVID pandemic did not trigger a worldwide reset, it imparted valuable lessons. It underscored the fragility of our societies and reinforced our interdependence. Humans thrive on narratives and models that guide and unite them toward a common purpose. Over recent history, various models have been tested in our global society. While fascism was evil and communism proved impractical, capitalism, too, has now exhibited its limitations.

The International Monetary Fund's (IMF) definition of capitalism underscores the pursuit of profit as its essence, alongside individualism. Capitalism encourages individuals to act in their economic self-interest, focusing on personal achievement and championing meritocracy. It asserts that individualistic capitalism promotes economic development by fostering good governance.

However, the practical application of capitalism often diverges from its ideal. Many companies primarily gauge their success by stock prices, subjecting themselves to the relentless pressure for growth. Yet, it's mathematically implausible to continue depleting finite resources for infinite growth.

Nate Hagens insightfully observes that our economy is a subsidiary of our environment. The relentless pursuit of GDP growth overshoots Earth's carrying capacity, leading to the depletion of vital resources, such as topsoil and water, and contributing to the ever-visible climate change disasters we witness daily. But the path to addressing climate change and other global challenges remains unclear.

In our collective frustration with the world's problems, some point accusatory fingers at corporations, especially multinational entities. Naomi Klein's *No Logo* has become their manifesto. But are all corporations inherently malevolent?

According to Professor Michael Porter, the primary role of business is wealth creation. Businesses achieve this by identifying needs, producing products or services, and selling them at a profit, which is then reinvested. There's no need to be ashamed of this fact, as only profitable businesses can contribute taxes and create jobs, both directly and indirectly. Moreover, a thriving business necessitates a thriving community; the two are intrinsically connected.

Issues like climate change, inequality, and gender balance frequently dominate the headlines, and rightfully so. Consequently, awareness of societal challenges has reached unprecedented levels. Yet, too often, businesses are perceived as part of the problem, not the solution. This perception must change and companies need to also adjust and reinvent their business model, especially as the younger generation seeks companies with a broader sense of purpose, extending beyond maximizing shareholder value.

Historically, business responses to societal challenges took the form of philanthropy, evolving into corporate social responsibility, then advancing further to concepts like Creating Shared Value or Net Zero. Simultaneously, the investment world embraced ESG (Environmental, Social, and Governance), leading to the emergence of B Corp accreditation.

However, these models, at their core, are all variations of capitalism. It's time to shift our perspective, acknowledging that societal challenges are not externalities necessitating government regulation to compel action. Social costs are intrinsically linked to business costs, and addressing societal needs should provide a sense of purpose.

Looking beyond individual companies, we must consider the entire ecosystem. NGOs highlight the issues, governments establish the infrastructure for businesses to create shared value, and businesses, encompassing suppliers and institutions, devise profitable solutions to meet these needs.

For businesses to flourish, they require effective governance, with a balanced board of directors playing three distinct roles: shareholders investing for a return, directors championing the company's promise, and managers bringing that promise to life through daily operations. In the eyes of the law, a company is a legal entity, and effective business governance hinges on maintaining the right balance between risk and return. But the legal entity, a person in the eyes of the law, is inanimate and incapacitated. It is the senior leadership of the company who are its conscience.

Consequently, the managers of a business should not exclusively focus on managing the profit and loss statement. Instead, they should adopt a customer-centric approach, with financial success naturally following. Unfortunately, the pressure from Wall Street often compels many business leaders to prioritize short-term gains over addressing societal needs.

Businesses and corporations are not inherently malevolent. Instead, we lack a collective sense of purpose and a systematic roadmap, hindering the collaboration necessary to tackle global issues. To navigate these challenges, we must harness both intelligence and wisdom. Capitalism has undeniably catalyzed global progress and lifted vast populations out of poverty. However, it now grapples with its inherent limitations.

What we need is a post-growth enlightenment, a global reset. Achieving this is no small feat. Our world currently operates within an intricately interdependent system with global supply chains, ensuring the delivery of essential goods, services, and luxuries we all desire.

While COVID-19 delivered an unmistakable global shock that impacted every corner of the planet, we've recently witnessed other disruptions, such as the semiconductor crisis and the ongoing conflict in Ukraine. These events revealed the vulnerability of our systems. Crafting a new path forward is essential, one that gradually decouples economic growth and well-being from the exhaustive use of finite resources.

The discourse surrounding technology's role in solving global issues is multifaceted, with divergent perspectives on its reach and efficacy. I will explore these nuances further in this book.

Initiating a Debate for Solutions

To catalyze meaningful change, we must move beyond acknowledgment to action. This section advocates for the initiation of a robust and inclusive debate—a platform where diverse perspectives converge to shape the narrative of change. It's a call to arms, urging stakeholders from all sectors to engage in a constructive dialogue that transcends boundaries. Furthermore, it outlines the importance of not just identifying problems but presenting tangible solutions that can pave the way for a sustainable future.

As we navigate through the urgency of change, these sections set the stage for a profound exploration of the transformative journey that lies ahead. Through collective understanding, shared vision, and actionable solutions, we can pave the way for a new era of sustainable business practices, anchored by the principles of the Ubuntu Polder Framework.

In our fast-paced, interconnected world, it has become imperative to ignite a global dialogue and propose solutions to address the multifaceted challenges that we face. We must come together, individuals from diverse backgrounds, to shape a collective narrative that not only guides our leaders but also inspires the general public to take coordinated and positive action. The urgency of the times is evident, but it's vital to remember a simple yet powerful Dutch saying, "Nee heb je, ja kun je krijgen," which translates to "You already have a no, and you might get a yes if you try." With this mantra in mind, I am wholeheartedly committed to participating in a constructive conversation, contributing my unique perspective to the narrative, and initiating a global dialogue.

"Geen woorden maar daden," which translates to "Not words but deeds," underscores the urgency of our time. Our planet's time is limited, and the need for action is pressing. It's akin to the saying that the best time to plant a tree was 20 years ago, and the second-best time is now. I firmly embrace this notion and believe that now is the moment for me to engage in a worldwide conversation about our shared future, before it's too late.

While it may seem that the world is in turmoil, there's no denying that something is undeniably amiss with our global socio-political-economic system. The signs are all around us, with more frequent economic downturns, political conflicts, food insecurity, migrant crisis, ecosystem collapse, and the accompanying human anxiety and suffering. Change is inevitable as finite resources become scarcer. However, the 'how' and 'when' of this change are within our control, and I am fully dedicated to being part of the solution, engaging in meaningful dialogue and taking action.

One fundamental question in today's business context is whether doing good inherently means lower profits. Figures like Prof. Gunther Pauli have started addressing this question, pushing forward the debate for alternative models. I've had the privilege of working with him on multiple projects and highly recommend his books. He advocates for the Blue Economy approach, which integrates circularity with profit and planet-oriented objectives. This approach mirrors the natural world, where waste in one process serves as the input for the next – a model we must learn from, be inspired by, and observe. Business, in essence, plays a vital role as a force for good by solving societal issues, creating jobs, uplifting communities, and restoring nature, as beautifully described by G. Pauli: Natural Value Creation and Community.

HOLISTIC IMPACT

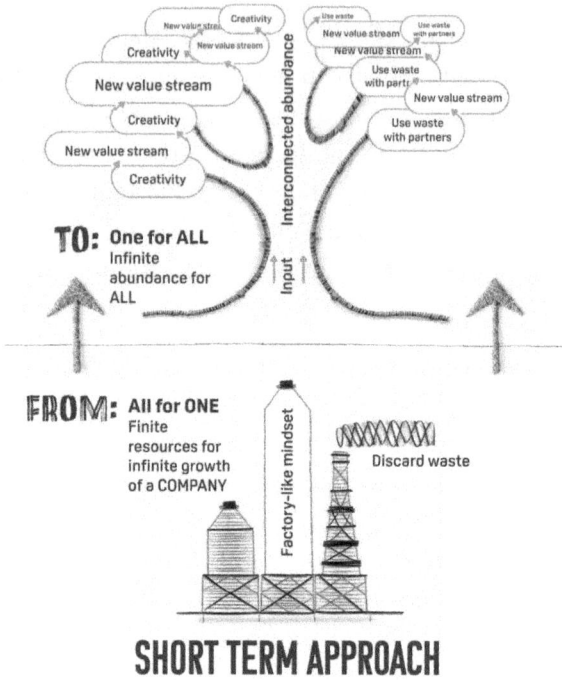

TO: One for ALL
Infinite abundance for ALL

FROM: All for ONE
Finite resources for infinite growth of a COMPANY

Discard waste

SHORT TERM APPROACH

The wisdom of figures like Paul Polman, former CEO of Unilever, also contributes to a more humane approach to business, as outlined in his book "Net Positive." His successful efforts to transform Unilever into a more responsible force for good are inspiring.

I aim to add my perspective to this dialogue by building upon the work of Professor Pauli, Paul Polman, and many others. This book serves as my contribution, like a pebble creating ripples in a pond, with the hope of intersecting with the ideas of others. I strive to promote conscious leadership, generating jobs, uplifting communities, and restoring nature.

While we can readily agree on the need for a new alternative model, the status quo often resists change. To find inspiration and leadership, we should consider the perspective of Frederick

Haren, who notes that those in developing countries are often more inclined to dream big and believe in the realization of their dreams. In a world that perceives many things as yet to be done, possibilities are limitless and attainable.

We must move away from the "not invented here" mentality and, much like in the developing world, embrace what works and build upon it. Global sense-making and collaboration are essential. Having spent most of my career in the developing world, I share Haren's perspective and appreciate the spirit of innovation, openness, and experimentation that is prevalent in such environments. In our quest for a better future, these qualities are invaluable.

The time for meaningful dialogue and positive action is now, and I am committed to playing my part in shaping a more sustainable and equitable world.

I don't claim to possess all the answers for the future or a comprehensive analysis of the past and present. However, I aim to share how I arrived at my personal insights and "aha" moments, in the hope that they will assist you in finding your own. The world's challenges can often appear overwhelming, leaving us with a sense of hopelessness and insignificance. Yet, whether we realize it or not, we are integral parts of a larger system, a part of humankind, and our individual actions trigger a chain reaction. Our pebble in the pond creates ripples that intertwine with others, producing unforeseen consequences. We have the power to choose the pebbles we throw, standing on the shoulders of those who came before us. In an individual's life, we experience five distinct phases:

1. The first 1,000 days, from pregnancy to two years of age.
2. 5,000 days of rapid growth during our teenage years.
3. 10,000 days as a young adult.
4. 10,000 days in middle age.
5. 10,000 days as a senior citizen.

These days amount to roughly 4,000 weeks, and the question posed by Oliver Burkeman in his book, *Four Thousand Weeks: Time Management for Mortals,* is crucial: How will you choose to make the most of them?

I want to emphasize once more that it's not about who is right or wrong but about how we handle differences. Open and constructive debate is essential in our digital age, steering us away from the destructive polarization that has become prevalent on Web 2.0 platforms. The current state of social media and the web, in general, demands substantial adjustments to promote empathy, understanding, and a more balanced presentation of the world's diverse perspectives.

The promise of Web 3.0 lies in its potential to bring about these fundamental corrections, fostering a more harmonious digital environment. It is hoped that this next evolution of the web will prioritize information sharing and interaction that transcends echo chambers, encouraging individuals to engage with a wide array of viewpoints and fostering a deeper sense of connection and unity. With the advent of Web 3.0, we envision a digital space that empowers individuals to embrace a holistic understanding of the world, ultimately mitigating the divisions and extreme polarization we have witnessed on Web 2.0.

We must ensure diverse perspectives and steer clear of groupthink.

Each of us is making a difference in our own way, and I have chosen to believe that I can have a meaningful impact, striving to maximize my positive influence by making it a habit to break my routines. I explored this topic in my presentation at the Conscious Companies' Summit 2022, titled "Geen woorden maar daden" (Not words but deeds).

Where Did I Get My Inspiration From?

In contemplating the driving force behind my mission and the Ubuntu Polder Framework for Business, I often find inspiration from my country of birth, the Netherlands. It is a nation that has achieved global prominence despite its diminutive size, limited land, and relatively small population. I attribute much of its success to the fact that it consists in large part of polders, land reclaimed from the sea, which requires constant pumping of water and maintenance of the dikes. Different societies living in the same polder have been forced throughout time to cooperate to avoid flooding. Whether you are rich or poor, male or female, or of any religion, when the dikes break, everyone is affected. This collaborative approach is often referred to as the "Polder model."

The Dutch model offers a profound lesson for the world's complex issues. Challenges of today are too intricate for any single entity, be it an institution, business, organization, or NGO, to address in isolation. We all find ourselves in the same polder: a single shared world facing a common adversary in the form of climate change. Our current economic model, which relies on Finite Resources for Infinite Growth, must undergo transformation, embracing greater Circularity that leverages local resources for sustained, interconnected abundance.

This shift may seem straightforward in principle, but it necessitates a fresh approach. We must move away from the linear, factory-like mindset and adopt holistic thinking. Collaboration with partners beyond our individual organizations is essential, forming ecosystems united by a common purpose and mutual benefit. Our goal should be to infuse circularity into all our endeavors, making efficient use of all waste. While not all waste may be processed or repurposed by the same company, let's at least establish transparency regarding the types and quantities of waste we generate, along with their regularity, and then seek connections with other businesses and communities.

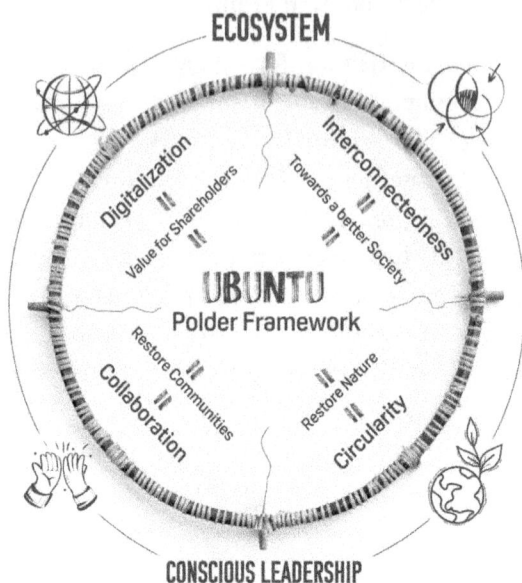

ECOSYSTEM

Digitalization

Interconnectedness

Value for Shareholders

Towards a better Society

UBUNTU
Polder Framework

Restore Communities

Restore Nature

Collaboration

Circularity

CONSCIOUS LEADERSHIP

To bridge the gaps between these diverse value streams, we should embrace and harness technology. Technology becomes the catalyst for transformation, for identifying the right partners, and for addressing challenges where solutions are not yet evident. The constant questioning, the "What If..." inquiry, plays a pivotal role. What if we could repurpose what we currently consider worthless? We can crowdsource solutions and leverage collective intelligence.

One prominent organization working to bring together governments, businesses, and civil society to address global issues is The World Economic Forum. I had the privilege to attend the WEF Africa in 2019, and during one discussion about Malaria eradication, a panelist astutely noted, "We need the affected countries to work together because mosquitoes don't have passports." Although it may sound like a jest, this observation carries a profound truth: our world is singular, our challenges are substantial, and they transcend borders, much like mosquitoes.

Drawing inspiration once more from the Polder model, we see the Dutch's innovative and creative spirit at work. They harnessed the resources at their disposal and refused to be limited by constraints. They embraced various forms of technology, whether in the conceptual realm, such as inventing banking, companies, and stock exchanges, or in practical tools like windmills that efficiently pumped water from the polder over the dikes and back into the sea, or the use of glasshouses to maintain optimal conditions for crop cultivation.

This model necessitates that leaders not only focus on what we commonly refer to as Lagging Key Performance Indicators (KPIs), which represent end results, but also pay equal attention to Leading KPIs – the 'how' of achieving these results. In essence, the world requires leaders who prioritize 'leading' rather than 'lagging.' Conscious leadership underscores the importance of 'how,' making it clear that it is not merely a superficial concept but an essential element for establishing genuine trust. I will unveil the formula for trust, demonstrating how focus on the greater good and reduced self-orientation fosters this trust. This, in turn, results in psychological safety, enabling the extraction of the best from your employees and partners within your ecosystem. Because whether we like it or not we are all connected and our success will only be sustainable if our communities and society are healthy. In other words we must be conscious of the spirit of Ubuntu: I am because we are.

In this book, I will recount my personal "aha" moments and the journey that led me to formulate what I now refer to as the Ubuntu Polder Framework for Business. I have lived and breathed this approach throughout my career in various countries, roles, and scales, and I will illustrate my insights through personal experiences.

Throughout this book, I will provide concrete examples and case studies of how I built meaningful ecosystems that lead to thriving together and create real win-win situations that can last.

What makes this model particularly attractive is that it doesn't necessitate a sudden overhaul of your business practices. Instead, it encourages you to start small, experiment, learn, fine-tune, and, when you've perfected it, confidently scale up. Nail it, then scale it.

In the subsequent chapters of this book, I will delve deeper into the practical application of the Ubuntu Polder Framework, offering insights, case studies, and actionable steps that can help transform businesses into forces for good.

THREE

THE UBUNTU POLDER FRAMEWORK: AFRICAN WISDOM AND DUTCH INGENUITY IN BUSINESS

CRAFTING THE POLDER FRAMEWORK BLUEPRINT

In the intricate dance of global business, where cultural nuances and diverse philosophies converge, the Ubuntu Polder Framework emerges as a synthesis of African wisdom and Dutch ingenuity. This chapter peels back the layers, unveiling the core components that make this model a beacon of transformative leadership.

The Ingredients of a Polder Model

Dutch Polders

At the heart of the Ubuntu Polder Framework lies a rich tapestry of ingredients, carefully woven together to create a harmonious and sustainable approach to business transformation. Drawing inspiration from African communal values and Dutch pragmatism, this section explores the unique elements that form the foundation of the Ubuntu Polder Framework. It's not just a theoretical framework; it's a living, breathing embodiment of interconnectedness and collaboration.

I've coined the model I aim to introduce as the Ubuntu Polder Framework, consisting of three fundamental elements: a commitment to collaborative endeavors for the greater good while ensuring businesses remain profitable.

There's a well-known Dutch saying, "God created the world, and the Dutch crafted the Netherlands," particularly in reference to the lowlands. This statement holds true, as nearly 50% of the Netherlands lies below sea level. In other words, half of the landmass is situated in polders, which are reclaimed lands. Achieving this involved encircling a piece of marshland, essentially a swamp, with dikes, thus transforming it into a polder. Windmills were constructed on these dikes to pump water from the polder back to the sea.

While I intend to use the Polder Framework as a metaphor, allow me to provide some additional context without delving into a detailed history lesson on the Netherlands.

In fact, the advent of the first windmills in the Netherlands marked the onset of the first Industrial Revolution. Initially, the Dutch employed this new technology to grind grain or corn into flour. Prior to this invention, grinding was done manually, followed by the use of horsepower with a treadmill, then watermills, before windmills took over in a country characterized by its flat, windy landscape. The operation of a windmill is straightforward. The windmill's cap is rotated from the ground, positioning the sails to face the wind. Wind energy is then harnessed to power the grain grinder.

During the period when the Dutch began erecting windmills, the western part of the Netherlands mainly consisted of marshlands and was scarcely habitable. The initial settlers in this region established their homes on local sand dunes to stay above the water level. With time and an increasing number of settlers, the inhabitants desired to live on the fertile soils surrounding the rapidly growing cities of Western Netherlands. Consequently, they constructed dikes to keep the water at bay. However, this gave rise to a new predicament: the need to drain groundwater and rainwater from the land within the dikes and discharge it into the river beyond to prevent the polders from flooding once more.

The governmental bodies responsible for managing polders, known as the District Water Boards, have their roots in the thirteenth century when they were established for water management. The founding of these Water Boards by Count Floris V marked a significant stride toward the development of modern democracy in the Netherlands. In those times, the primary concern was the ebb and flow of water, but the Water Boards necessitated a collaborative commitment from all residents to collectively work towards maintaining dry lands.

Nevertheless, despite strenuous efforts, a catastrophic event occurred in 1421 – the devastating Saint Elizabeth's Flood. This calamity claimed the lives of hundreds of thousands as it inundated numerous villages. The infamous Saint Elizabeth's flood was a result of the inadequate maintenance of the dikes safeguarding the polder. Following the occurrence of the disaster, a pivotal breakthrough emerged when they conceived the notion of employing windmills for water pumping. They harnessed the energy of the wind, but instead of driving a millstone, it powered a water wheel that lifted the water up by 1.5 meters. These water-windmills played a crucial role in draining the polders, channeling the water into the canals. As the canals filled during the ebb tide, the sluices would open their gates, releasing the excess water in the direction of the natural river and the sea. This ingenious system effectively managed water levels in the region.

The miller was responsible for the windmill's operation and often resided in the windmill with their entire family. Despite their significant role in society, millers did not earn substantial incomes. Millers' wives frequently sought additional employment because the miller needed to remain close to the mill, and windmills were often situated in remote locations.

During the 19th century, windmills reached their zenith in the Netherlands, with a total of 10,000 in operation. However, as technological advancements led to the invention of the steam engine and, later, electricity, windmills began to be gradually replaced by powered pumping stations. This transition aimed to reduce dependence on natural elements like wind and enhance efficiency.

Today, only 1,200 windmills remain in the Netherlands, with many serving as backups and still fully functional, showcasing the enduring legacy of this iconic Dutch innovation.

The significance of windmills in water management is widely recognized, and Dutch society holds a deep fascination for these iconic structures. In a testament to their importance, former Queen and the mother of the current King of the Netherlands, Princess Beatrix, serves as the patroness of the Dutch Windmill Association.

The windmills played a crucial role in draining the polder, and canals and dikes completed the process. Every member of society, from the humble miller to the country's monarch, contributes in various capacities, all indispensable to sustain the Polder model.

I spent my formative years in a polder, where the ever-present threat of disaster underscored the importance of vigilance, having contingency plans, and fostering a spirit of cooperation.

African Wisdom: Understanding Ubuntu

In the Zulu language of South Africa, the term "Ubuntu" embodies the concept of "Humanity." It is often translated as "I am because we are" or "Humanity towards others." At a more profound level, Ubuntu represents the belief in a universal bond of sharing that unites all of humanity. According to the African Journal of Social Work, Ubuntu can be defined as a collection of values and practices that people of African descent use to shape authentic human beings. Although the specific nuances of these values and practices may vary among different ethnic groups, they all point to a central idea - that an authentic individual human being is inherently connected to a broader, more significant world that includes relationships, community, society, environment, and spirituality.

Ubuntu underscores the interdependence of humans on each other and the recognition of one's responsibility to their fellow humans and the world at large. It is a philosophy that prioritizes collectivism over individualism.

However, Ubuntu is not merely an abstract theory found in books or magazines; it is deeply ingrained and experienced in the daily lives of people in Africa. One powerful story that beautifully illustrates the concept of Ubuntu involves a Western anthropologist who came to Africa many years ago to study the way of life of African ethnic groups.

During his work with African children, the anthropologist organized a game. He placed a basket filled with sweet fruits beneath a Baobab tree and gathered all the children around. He challenged them to stand 100 meters away from the tree, explaining that the first child to reach the basket would get to keep it all. What transpired next left the anthropologist astounded. Instead of competing individually, the children joined hands and ran together toward the tree. As a result, they reached the basket together and joyfully shared the fruits.

This story encapsulates the essence of Ubuntu: "I am what I am because of who we all are." It exemplifies the spirit of unity, cooperation, and interconnectedness that lies at the heart of this profound African philosophy.

A Circular Approach: Unlocking Multiple Revenue Streams

In the song "St. Stephen" by the Grateful Dead, there's a line that resonates deeply: "One man gathers what another man spills." Since the 1960s, this band has been a source of inspiration for environmental activists. For me, this line encapsulates the essence of circularity and points toward the future of our global model. We should shift from linear production models to embrace circularity, mirroring nature's ability to produce with minimal waste. Circular thinking holds the potential to address numerous global challenges, fostering sustainability, job creation, and the cultivation of additional revenue streams while efficiently utilizing and reutilizing finite resources to become infinite.

However, the transition is no simple task and requires unconventional thinking and the courage to challenge established business norms. A critical principle of the circular economy is to initiate projects with a solid return on investment from the outset, generating employment opportunities and strengthening local economies. By approaching value chains from a fresh perspective and thinking outside the box, new opportunities come to light. For instance, realizing that only 0.2% of the biomass of a coffee plant ends up in a cup of coffee prompts the question: What if we could utilize the other 99.8%? I will share how in South Africa, we harnessed this unused biomass to cultivate mushrooms, simultaneously creating jobs.

Professor G. Pauli encourages us to break free from the confines of conventional thinking and to persistently explore beyond the obvious, never returning to the restrictive "box." Our actions should be directed toward making a positive difference, a tried-and-true recipe for greater happiness. It involves embracing the "Art de Vivre" - the art of living - and becoming more sensitive and creative, much like the natural world. This approach promotes a richer, more fulfilling existence that aligns with the harmony found in nature.

The Ubuntu Polder Framework is a forward-thinking and comprehensive approach to business transformation that promotes cooperation, interconnectedness, and sustainable practices. It takes full advantage of the latest technology and embraces the digital economy to generate its revenues by solving societal needs. It's particularly relevant in today's business world as it addresses the pressing need for responsible, holistic, and value-driven business models.

The Ubuntu Polder Framework in Summary

Ubuntu Philosophy:

Interconnectedness: Ubuntu is an African philosophy that emphasizes the interconnectedness of all life. In the context of business, it means understanding how a company's actions impact its ecosystem, including the environment, society, and stakeholders.

Polder Framework Influence: Cooperation and Consensus: The Polder Framework is a Dutch approach to decision-making characterized by social dialogue, cooperation, and consensus. It has been adapted to the Ubuntu Polder Framework to stress the importance of collaboration among stakeholders.

PRINCIPLES IN ACTION AND ROADMAP INSIGHTS

To truly understand the essence of the Ubuntu Polder Framework, we delve into its key principles. These principles, shaped by the wisdom of Ubuntu and the pragmatic approach of the Dutch Polder Model, provide a compass for leaders navigating the complexities of the modern business landscape. Each principle is a guiding star, steering organizations towards a holistic transformation that transcends mere profitability.

Stakeholder Value Creation: The model focuses on creating value for all stakeholders, not just shareholders. It recognizes that a successful business should benefit employees, customers, suppliers, communities, and the environment. It cares and connects people internally as well as in its whole value chain and turns these connections into a functioning ecosystem.

Societal Needs and Rewards: Instead of merely pursuing profit, the Ubuntu Polder Framework encourages businesses to address societal needs and get rewarded for doing so. This aligns with the idea of business as a force for good.

Restoring Nature: The model promotes environmental responsibility, emphasizing the need to restore and protect nature. It's aligned with sustainability and circularity goals.

Employment Creation: By addressing societal needs and adopting sustainable practices, businesses can also contribute to employment generation, which is a critical aspect of societal well-being.

Resource Efficiency: The model encourages resource efficiency and minimizing waste, which is in line with circular economy principles. It furthermore uses its waste to generate new revenue streams.

Community Engagement: Engaging with local communities and understanding their needs is vital for building trust and a positive social impact.

It embraces and incorporates technology and digital.

Transparency and Accountability: Governance and ethical behavior are paramount. Businesses must be transparent about their actions and be accountable for their impact on society and the environment.

Relevance in Today's Business World

In a world characterized by rapid change and increasing inter-connectedness, the relevance of the Ubuntu Polder Framework becomes more pronounced than ever. This section explores how this model is not just a relic of the past or a utopian vision but a practical, timely response to the challenges businesses face today. It's a roadmap for sustainability, resilience, and meaningful impact in a dynamically evolving global economy.

Sustainability: The Ubuntu Polder Framework aligns with the global sustainability movement. In a world facing environmental challenges, businesses that embrace sustainability are more likely to thrive.

ESG and Stakeholder Capitalism: The model is aligned with the growing focus on Environmental, Social, and Governance (ESG) criteria. Stakeholder capitalism, which prioritizes the interests of all stakeholders, is becoming more mainstream.

Circular Economy: Circular business models, which emphasize resource efficiency and waste reduction, resonate with the Ubuntu Polder Framework's approach to circularity.

Societal Expectations: Consumers, investors, and governments increasingly expect businesses to operate responsibly and make a positive impact on society.

Long-Term Value: By creating a holistic, responsible business model, companies can enhance their long-term value, reputation, and resilience.

Competitive Advantage: Adopting the Ubuntu Polder Framework can provide a unique selling proposition and a competitive advantage, especially for businesses looking to differentiate themselves.

In summary, the Ubuntu Polder Framework advocates a business approach that's both ethical and future-focused. It acknowledges the need for businesses to be responsible, sustainable, and deeply connected with their ecosystems and communities. In today's evolving business landscape, where societal and environmental concerns are paramount, the Ubuntu Polder Framework offers a visionary pathway for businesses to thrive while contributing positively to the world.

The Key Pillars of the Ubuntu Polder Framework for Business

Building upon the principles, we unveil the key pillars that sustain the Ubuntu Polder Framework. These pillars, rooted in collaboration, environmental consciousness, and social responsibility, form the structural foundation of a business model that goes beyond profit margins. Understanding and embracing these pillars is pivotal for organizations aspiring to embody the Ubuntu Polder Framework in their ethos.

Personal Commitment and the Right Mindset Leading to Action

The Ubuntu Polder Framework - The Path to Holistic Business Transformation:

In our exploration of the Ubuntu Polder Framework and its application in achieving holistic business transformation, we must begin with a fundamental formula for change. This formula, which I consider the cornerstone of our journey, can be summarized as follows: Experience + Knowledge + Action (and a healthy dose of time for reflection) = Result/Change. It's the blueprint that encapsulates my journey and the philosophy that underlies the transformative power of this model.

However, it's essential to understand that the transformative journey doesn't start with action; it starts with cultivating the right mindset and belief. Before we take any action, there are critical steps that precede it. These initial steps are personal commitment, prioritizing, persistence, and the formation of productive habits.

Personal Commitment: The Catalyst for Change

The first and foremost element in our formula is personal commitment. This is the point at which you make a conscious decision to embark on a journey of transformation. In my case, this commitment led me to establish Ubuntu in Dubai, a consultancy and advisory company committed to reshaping the business world. The core belief behind this commitment is that business can be a force for good and a catalyst for positive change.

Prioritizing: Aligning with Your Values: Once the commitment is made, the next step is prioritizing. This involves aligning your actions and decisions with the values and principles that resonate with your vision. In my own journey, I prioritized sustainability, circularity, digital, and ESG principles at the heart of doing business. These priorities became my guiding lights, influencing my choices and actions.

Persistence: The Steadfast Pursuit of Change: Holistic transformation is not a swift process. It requires persistence and unwavering dedication. Drawing from my experiences as an international expat in various parts of the world, I learned that persistence is key. It's about staying the course, especially in the face of challenges and setbacks, which are inevitable in the business landscape.

Habits: Embedding Transformation in Your Culture: To ensure that your commitment and persistence yield sustainable change, it's crucial to develop habits that reflect your values. This means creating a corporate culture that embraces the principles of sustainability, circularity, and ESG. The Ubuntu Polder Framework is not just a concept; it's a set of ingrained habits that guide every decision and action within the organization.

Now that we've set the foundation with these crucial elements, we can delve deeper into the power of the right mindset and belief, which serve as the driving forces behind personal commitment, prioritizing, persistence, and habits.

Personal Commitment and the Right Mindset Leading to Action: Suzuki Roshi's wise words, "You're perfect exactly as you are (and you could use a little work)," remind us that our mindset is pivotal in shaping our lives. In a world where distractions are abundant, and it's easy to get lost in daily routines and endless scrolling on our smartphones, it's imperative to shift our perspective. We should focus on what we want to achieve, learn, explore, and know more about. By planning our time and dedicating even a small portion of our day to these pursuits, we can witness significant progress. Forming this habit may require initial effort, often cited as around 21 days of persistent and uninterrupted dedication, but it eventually becomes second nature, laying the groundwork for meaningful action.

Our mindset, in particular, plays a paramount role because our beliefs guide our behavior. A positive mindset is a game-changer. I recall my early career days, where I had the privilege of learning from seasoned professionals. One of the senior leaders, Lim King Fung, shared invaluable wisdom, advising me to "keep smiling" for a successful career. Although it puzzled me initially, I later realized that his message was about radiating positive energy. Over time, I delved deeper into the virtues of a positive mindset, discovering the profound impact of Positive Intelligence, which involves seeking the positive and seizing opportunities in every situation.

In performance evaluations with my staff, I always allocate time for feedback on our working relationship. I vividly remember one of my staff members providing insightful feedback: "Your energy rubs off on me and makes me want to do more and do better." It reinforced the wisdom of Lim King Fung's advice.

Our society often emphasizes the importance of possessions, leading to a "have-do-be" approach, where we believe that we must first possess something, then take actions to achieve, and only then can we be happy or fulfilled. However, Chris Peter advocates for reversing this order to "be-do-have." In this revised approach, you start by believing and being content with what you already have, which informs your behavior. Your actions are then rewarded with what you desire.

This concept aligns with the growth mindset principle, a timeless approach that can be traced back to Rumi in the 13th century, who encouraged living as if everything is rigged in your favor. Belief leads to action, and without action, nothing is accomplished. In business, it's often said that a vision without action is a dream, action without vision is a nightmare, and a vision with action can change the world.

In all my teams, I have made it clear that I am a staunch believer in Positive Energy. Understanding the profound power of your thoughts reinforces the idea that negative thinking should be banished from your mind. As my friend Conn Bertish aptly puts it, "Happy people are harder to kill." Conn's personal journey fighting cancer through visualization and the power of the mind led him to create Cancer Dojo, an initiative aimed at helping children use their minds in their battle against cancer.

To overcome my own limiting paradigms, I adopted a personal mantra: "I am who I am; my knowledge is deep and wide, and I trust my instincts."

The journey toward a Positive Mindset opens doors that one cannot foresee. To illustrate this power, I'd like to share my wife Erma's story. When we met in Indonesia at the start of my career, she was studying dentistry. After our marriage, she embraced the expat lifestyle, which posed challenges for her dental career due to frequent relocations. Her journey took her from practicing dentistry in Vietnam to studying fashion design at the University of LaSalle in the Philippines. In Switzerland, where in order to work as a dentist a further French language proficiency and a medical residency was required, she pursued fashion design further. Her exploration led her to discover the synergy between

African and Indonesian batik patterns, inspiring her to create Afrosia, a fusion of African and Indonesian-inspired fashion. Through determination and a positive mindset, she introduced her designs to the Miss Cameroon regional competition. Her creations were a hit, and this success marked the beginning of her remarkable journey. It eventually led her to become Vice-President of Miss Cameroon, where she managed to get, for the first time ever, Miss Cameroon to participate in the global Miss World Competition. In her efforts to increase cultural exchanges with Indonesia and showcase Cameroonian talent to the world, she organized a Music, Fashion, and Film Festival that brought international attention to Central and West African talents. Erma's story exemplifies the power of belief and action in achieving success.

In any field, knowledge and talent are important, but the key ingredients are determination, consistency, and persistence. This applies to your career, writing a book, learning a new language, and any other endeavor. Complacency is the enemy in a world that evolves rapidly, demanding continuous learning, unlearning, and relearning.

In a world that often feels rudderless and leaderless, it is crucial for us to envision a better world and believe that we can bring about positive change through our actions. Belief guides our actions, bringing us closer to this better world. Our thoughts have a creative power, both consciously and unconsciously. The most potent force is what we tell ourselves and believe. A mindset that recognizes our interconnectedness and embraces the philosophy of "I am because we are" and our strength in vulnerability is the path to a brighter, more abundant world. Let's support one another, building mutual self-esteem, trust, commitment, love, abundance, respect, and unity in our shared Polder, which must become our natural state, flowing effortlessly.

As Terence McKenna wisely noted, "Nature loves courage. You make the commitment, and nature will respond by removing seemingly insurmountable obstacles." When you dare to dream the impossible dream, the world won't crush you; it will lift you up. This is the secret, the understanding of all those remarkable teachers and philosophers who grasped the alchemical gold. It's the shamanic dance in the waterfall, the magic of hurling yourself into the abyss and discovering it's a feather bed.

In challenging times, it's essential to remember that an airplane takes off against the wind, not with it, as Henry Ford wisely observed. Real change begins with self-transformation. It's a simple equation: Experience + Knowledge + Action = Results/Change. Every remarkable journey starts with that first step. This concept is logical and straightforward, yet we often procrastinate and wait for others to act. The individuals who truly make an impact, those we admire, are the ones who take action. They readily admit to their numerous mistakes and frequent failures before achieving success. The formula is clear: start, stumble, continue experimenting, observe, refine, and persist until you feel you've mastered it. Then, and only then, should you move forward to scale it.

Now, let's incorporate the importance of being discerning in what you say yes to, ensuring that your actions are meaningful and worth your time.

Being Discerning in Your Actions

In the journey of personal commitment and the right mindset leading to action, it's crucial to be discerning in what you say yes to. Your actions should align with your goals and resonate with your values. Consider three types of "yes" responses:

IQ (Mind) – Logical Alignment: Ensure that your actions make logical sense and align with your goals and objectives. Will they contribute to your long-term vision and mission?

EQ (Heart) – Emotional Connection: Consider the emotional aspect. Do these actions strengthen your relationships and connections with others? Will they enhance your collaborative efforts and create positive team dynamics?

BQ (Gut/Body) – Intuitive Harmony: Listen to your intuition. Does it feel right deep in your gut? Is there a sense of comfort, or does it raise discomfort? Trust your instincts when making decisions.

By discerning and aligning your actions with your intellect, emotions, and intuition, you ensure that your efforts are purposeful and meaningful. This discernment is essential in the journey of transformation, helping you direct your energy and resources toward actions that truly matter. For all critical issues and decisions, ensure to get three times a Yes, when asking does it make sense to the Head, Heart and Gut, before moving forward.

In this chapter, we've explored the formula for change, the role of personal commitment, the power of a positive mindset, and the importance of being discerning in your actions. These elements are the building blocks of the Ubuntu Polder Framework, which empowers businesses to become forces for good in the world. The path to holistic business transformation is illuminated, and we are ready to embark on a journey that can change the world for the better.

Cultivate Cooperation and Gain Buy-in within your Organization

Once your mindset as a leader is clear and ready for action, the next critical step is to align your entire organization with your vision. This alignment requires dedicated work on the company culture, as it is the driving force behind successful execution. Here, we'll explore the concrete example of how this can be achieved.

While personal commitment is vital, it's equally crucial to bring the entire team on board. To achieve this, having a clear direction or compelling vision is critical. This not only serves to inspire people but also provides a practical framework. A compelling vision allows you to break down the overarching goal into three or four distinct buckets or priorities, which can then be further divided into two or three achievable milestones. This systematic approach makes it less intimidating for team members to take action and get started. Remember, course correction is always an option. Putting this plan on paper also streamlines teamwork, as it illustrates the connections, clarifies each person's role, and allows everyone to work independently while moving in the same direction.

It's equally important to address and overcome the fears that often paralyze initiative. Fears of failure, concerns about falling out of favor with managers, or the dread of appearing foolish in front of peers can hinder progress. Of course, not every action will lead to success, especially in complex tasks involving multiple people. That's why it's essential to define the intended outcome as clearly as possible from the outset.

Additionally, fostering a culture of psychological safety is key. In this kind of culture, employees can bring their full selves to work without fear of judgment. It's a place where building on each other's ideas is encouraged, where small victories, and even intelligent failures, are celebrated as part of the journey towards progress.

Building a strong and healthy team culture is essential for a team's performance and effectiveness. Research suggests that there are three key elements that need to be developed and protected:

1. **Psychological Safety for Action:** Do team members feel safe expressing themselves, speaking up when they have questions or concerns, respectfully disagreeing with each other, and even making mistakes? It's important to distinguish between different

types of mistakes, such as silly and avoidable errors versus intelligent failures. Intelligent failures often lead to valuable learning experiences that propel the team in the right direction, increasing the likelihood of success. When team members can openly discuss without fear of judgment, diverse perspectives emerge, and people are more likely to voice their opinions and concerns before errors occur.

2. Common Goals for Cooperation: It's crucial for everyone on the team to understand how their individual expertise and responsibilities contribute to the team's overall performance and its place within the broader organizational context. When everyone is aligned around common objectives, it fosters cooperation and a shared sense of purpose.

3. Prosocial Purpose: Knowing the purpose of their work isn't enough; employees also want to understand who their work is serving. When team members recognize that their efforts are making a meaningful contribution to the world and positively impacting others, they experience a sense of prosocial purpose. This feeling, in turn, fuels collective focus and motivation, as the team works together towards a greater good.

By cultivating these three elements, you can create a team culture that not only performs well but also thrives, learns from its experiences, and stays committed to a shared mission.

In the corporate world, it is often easy to agree that the right team or company culture is important and even to determine the right values. However, leaders frequently do not spend enough time making this desired culture a lived reality on the ground. The culture is often defined during a top leadership retreat and becomes an abstract series of words and statements on paper.

In my role as the head of 23 countries in a newly formed region, I realized that I had to do better. Group dynamics do not naturally fall into alignment. Different silos create an "us and them" situation, both vertically and horizontally, leading to suboptimal engagement among employees. To make the culture concrete and tangible, we worked with a South African company called Blueprint.

Before engaging Blueprint, we already worked on the fundamentals of building our culture. I required the entire management team to practice "leadership at the shop floor." We held hundreds of town hall sessions covering all sites and geographies on a minimum quarterly basis. We focused on the conscious common thread of integration and inclusion, with the goal of bringing all employees together not just in their minds but also in their hearts. We emphasized building an organization where we care about each other's safety, where you can be yourself, where you are told what is really going on, where your strengths are magnified, where your daily work is rewarding, and where unnecessary rules do not exist.

With Blueprint, we co-created our culture with the involvement of over 95% of all employees, referring to it as our "winning formula." It started with leadership clarity on the "picture of success" but then asked the opinion of the entire organization, ensuring full inclusivity. This quantification led to an almost scientifically codified representation of the absolute truth of the current culture and discussion on the priority elements of the desired culture. It identified both the enablers (behaviors we want to see more of) and the disablers (behaviors we want to see less of).

This then got visualized by making an icon of each enabler and disabler. These icons were created by the employees themselves, making them deeply meaningful. The overall formula, with enablers on the top and disablers on the bottom, became a real piece of art. By displaying it in various locations, it served as a daily, tangible reminder, entering the consciousness and memories of all. Quarterly surveys allowed us to track the culture strength and trends across the organization and address potential hotspots proactively. Over time, we could even use culture as a predictor of which areas in the company would do well and which were likely to perform poorly. This approach turned what is traditionally seen as a "soft" factor into a "hard" element that drove performance.

Expand the Field and Create an Ecosystem

To achieve abundance and a brighter future, we must recognize that the path to success involves working together within a broader ecosystem. In this ecosystem, the idea of a win-win situation is clearly defined, where people and organizations come together in a gig economy approach.

In the 1930s, British botanist Arthur Tansley introduced the term "ecosystem" to describe a community of organisms interacting with each other and their environment, encompassing elements like air, water, and earth. Within this framework, organisms compete, collaborate, co-evolve, and adapt collectively to external changes in order to thrive.

This biological concept found a parallel in the world of business through the work of business strategist James Moore, who, in his 1993 *Harvard Business Review* article, "Predators and Prey: A New Ecology of Competition," likened companies in the increasingly interconnected world of commerce to a community of organisms adapting and evolving to survive. Moore proposed that businesses shouldn't be viewed in isolation but as members of a broader business ecosystem, spanning multiple industries.

In the context of advances in technology and globalization, the concept of a business ecosystem helps companies navigate the rapidly changing business landscape. Moore's definition of a business ecosystem encapsulates its essence:

"An economic community supported by a foundation of interacting organizations and individuals—the organisms of the business world. The economic community produces goods and services of value to customers, who are themselves members of the ecosystem. The member organisms also include suppliers, lead producers, competitors, and other stakeholders. Over time, they co-evolve their capabilities and roles and tend to align themselves with the directions set by one or more central companies. Those companies holding leadership roles may change over time, but the function of an ecosystem leader is valued by the community because it enables members to move toward shared visions, to align their investments, and to find mutually supportive roles."

In essence, a business ecosystem comprises a network of interconnected companies dynamically interacting through competition and cooperation to enhance sales and ensure survival. This network encompasses suppliers, distributors, consumers, government entities, processes, products, and competitors. A thriving ecosystem implies that participants have developed patterns of behavior that streamline the flow of ideas, talent, and capital throughout the system.

At its core, an ecosystem is a community of living organisms interacting in a specific environment. In the business context, it represents a purposeful arrangement between multiple entities (members) to create and share collective value for a common set of customers, often orchestrated by one member. This business ecosystem includes various stakeholders, from suppliers to customers, and is characterized by both competition and cooperation. Each entity within the ecosystem affects and is affected by the others, creating a constantly evolving relationship that demands flexibility and adaptability, much like a biological ecosystem.

This concept resonates with Ubuntu, where cooperation and interaction within the community lead to protection, prosperity, and the building of livelihoods, much like the Dutch Polders, which were miniature ecosystems. The Dutch government embraced this model, applying it to their governance approach by seeking the cooperation and buy-in of the public, private sectors, and labor before taking action. We see this ecosystem approach increasingly applied in the business world as the gig economy becomes a reality.

FUNCTIONING ECOSYSTEM

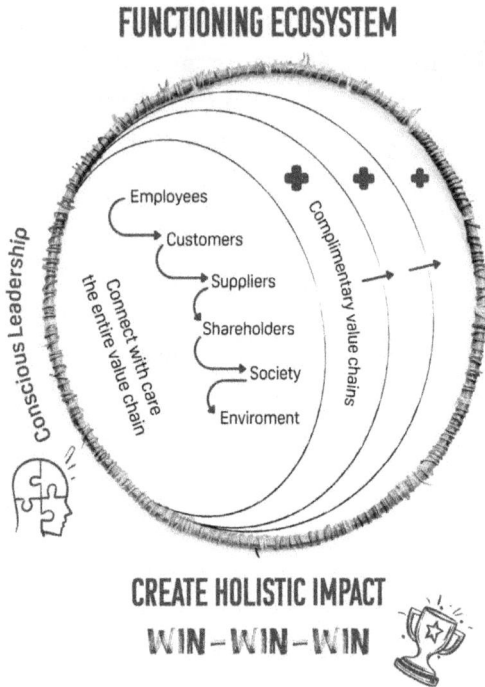

Employees
Customers
Suppliers
Shareholders
Society
Enviroment

Complimentary value chains

Connect with care the entire value chain

Conscious Leadership

CREATE HOLISTIC IMPACT
WIN – WIN – WIN

In today's world, the challenges we face are too complex and interconnected for any single entity, whether it's a government, business, or organization, to address on its own. Collaboration and leveraging each other's strengths and skills are necessary to be effective. This approach allows knowledge, wealth, and resources to multiply into abundance.

In practice, forming partnerships and ecosystems requires a clear definition of the benefits for everyone involved, ensuring a win-win situation from the outset to prevent disappointments and avoid the need for renegotiation.

Creating such ecosystems demands courage, vulnerability, strong communication skills, going above and beyond, and entrusting the team. It also necessitates a shift in mindset toward circularity, where resources and ideas circulate and multiply, fostering sustainable growth. Furthermore, modern technology plays a crucial role in coordinating and facilitating communication within these ecosystems, making them not just a possibility but a practical reality.

Think Society, Circularity, and Multiple Revenue Streams

Large multinational companies, often subject to criticism, are, in reality, continuously learning, adapting, and innovating, just like any other entity striving for survival. It's an imperative demand of our times. While local businesses may sometimes lack the resources, culture, knowledge, scale, and ambition needed to confront the challenges posed by climate change, these global giants possess the reach and influence to be pivotal in shaping a sustainable future. They can, and should, become a positive force for good, as an ecosystem leader and even acting as market creators.

However, it's crucial to understand that this cannot be achieved in isolation. To effectively address climate change and sustainability issues, large corporations must embrace an ecosystem approach and adopt circular economy thinking. Take, for instance, the significant amount of global drinking water and CO_2 emissions used in agriculture, at 75%, rather than industry, around 5%. Therefore, while these companies work on cleaning up their industrial manufacturing operations, they must extend their efforts beyond their own boundaries, actively engaging in collaborative efforts across the entire value chain.

This transformation calls for a fundamental shift in the way companies perceive and structure their business models. It cannot solely rely on the vision and willingness to change from the CEO alone; it requires a widespread understanding, buy-in, and a steadfast, long-term commitment that is consistently followed through.

However, when this transformation is successfully undertaken, the benefits are nothing short of extraordinary. The company begins to create revenues and generate value from multiple value streams. The ecosystem allows for a seamless integration of small entrepreneurial companies with much larger organizations. All employees within the organization feel a much stronger sense of purpose, knowing that real societal issues are being addressed, without generating waste but instead leading to abundance.

However, it is key to atone the obsession of only wanting to work on the so called "core competencies" of the company. We need to go beyond these narrowly defined core activities and be willing to create new value streams by using the waste created in new ways. You do this by working with partners who are more specialized in that area, creating an ecosystem.

In this Ubuntu Polder Framework, the emphasis is on creating a win-win-win scenario, where society benefits from sustainable practices, businesses thrive through multiple revenue streams and value creation, and the environment prospers as waste is minimized. It's a model that enables companies to operate with a more profound purpose, transcending the conventional profit-driven mindset, and instead, fostering a commitment to address the pressing challenges of our time. The result is a world where businesses act as agents of positive change, ecosystems function harmoniously, and abundance becomes the new norm.

Proposing the Ubuntu Polder Framework for Business

The Ubuntu Polder Framework I propose is influenced by my Dutch upbringing, shaped by my experiences in the developing world, and validated through my hands-on involvement. This model places a high value on individual awareness, the drive to take action and achieve, while also recognizing the imperative of cooperation and the creation of an ecosystem. It draws inspiration from nature's interdependence and aims to establish multiple revenue streams, ultimately leading to a win-win-win scenario for the company, society, and nature.

Operationalizing The Ubuntu Polder Framework requires a structured framework that includes an EcoSystem Scan, brainstorming sessions to identify projects and initiatives, and the essential step of equipping your team with the necessary skills.

Assessment Tool

To guide businesses on their transformative journey, an assessment tool becomes an invaluable companion. This section introduces a practical tool designed to evaluate an organization's alignment with the Ubuntu Polder Framework. It's more than a checklist; it's a diagnostic instrument that illuminates strengths, identifies areas for improvement, and catalyzes the introspection necessary for genuine transformation.

To assess the current state of a business in terms of Digital, Sustainability, Circularity, and ESG, you can create a comprehensive assessment tool with various criteria. Here are the key components:

1. Digital Transformation:

- *Technology Infrastructure:* Evaluate the existing tech stack, its efficiency, and its adaptability to future needs.

- *Data Analytics:* Assess data management, analytics capabilities, and data-driven decision-making.
- *Digital Strategy:* Review the alignment of digital initiatives with the overall business strategy.
- *Customer Experience:* Measure the digital touchpoints and customer satisfaction.
- *Digital Fitness of the Employees:* Evaluate the need to upskill your employees to feel more comfortable and not see the transformation with fear.

2. Sustainability:

- *Environmental Impact:* Analyze the company's carbon footprint, resource consumption, and waste management.
- *Sustainable Supply Chain:* Assess suppliers' sustainability practices and their impact on your business.
- *Eco-friendly Products/Services:* Evaluate the eco-friendliness of your offerings.
- *Regulatory Compliance:* Ensure compliance with environmental regulations.

3. Circularity:

- *Resource Efficiency:* Analyze how efficiently resources are used and identify areas for circularity.
- *Product Lifecycle:* Assess product design for recyclability and reusability.
- *Waste Reduction:* Evaluate waste management and recycling processes.
- *Circular Business Models:* Identify opportunities for circular business models.

4. ESG (Environmental, Social, and Governance):

- *Environmental:* Measure carbon emissions and environmental initiatives.
- *Social:* Assess diversity and inclusion, employee welfare, and community engagement.
- *Governance:* Evaluate corporate governance, ethics, and transparency.

5. Ecosystem and Value Chain Interaction:

- Analyze how your business interacts with suppliers, customers, and partners concerning Digital, Sustainability, Circularity, and ESG.
- Assess the impact on the broader community and stakeholders.

3-Step Roadmap

Navigating the path toward holistic business transformation requires a strategic roadmap. This chapter unveils a clear, actionable 3-step roadmap, offering a structured approach to implementing the Ubuntu Polder Framework. From initial conceptualization to full integration, each step is a deliberate move towards a business paradigm that prioritizes purpose alongside profit.

Once you've conducted the assessment, you can follow this three-step roadmap for transformation:

Step 1: Define and Prioritize Objectives

- Collaborate with the leadership team to define clear objectives for Digital, Sustainability, Circularity, and ESG.

- Prioritize these objectives based on impact and feasibility.

Step 2: Design a Holistic Transformation Plan

- Develop a comprehensive transformation plan that integrates Digital, Sustainability, Circularity, and ESG into the core business model.
- Set specific KPIs and milestones for each area.
- Ensure that the plan considers interactions with the ecosystem and value chain.

Step 3: Implementation and Continuous Improvement

- Execute the transformation plan, involving all relevant stakeholders.
- Monitor progress using the established KPIs.
- Continuously review and adjust the plan as necessary.
- Communicate progress and successes both internally and externally to build trust and engagement.

Remember that this transformation is an ongoing process. It requires commitment, resources, and a willingness to adapt to changing circumstances. The Ubuntu Polder Framework, which emphasizes cooperation and interconnectedness, will be valuable for this journey towards business as a force for good.

Roadmap: Transitioning from Business as Usual to Embracing the Ubuntu Polder Framework

1. Understanding Ubuntu Polder Framework Principles:

- *Assemble a Core Team:* Form a team dedicated to understanding the principles and nuances of the Ubuntu

Polder Framework. Include members from various departments to ensure diverse perspectives.

2. Educational Initiatives:

- *Training Programs:* Conduct workshops and training programs to educate employees at all levels about the Ubuntu Polder Framework, emphasizing its holistic approach to business transformation.

3. Leadership Alignment:

- *Engage Leadership:* Communicate with top leadership to secure their commitment to the Ubuntu Polder Framework. Ensure alignment with the model's values and objectives.

4. Assessment of Current Practices:

- *Holistic Business Review:* Evaluate existing business practices, identifying areas where the Ubuntu Polder Framework principles can be integrated seamlessly.

5. Stakeholder Engagement:

- *Identify Stakeholders:* Map out key stakeholders, including employees, customers, suppliers, and communities. Develop strategies for meaningful engagement and collaboration.

6. Circularity Integration:

- *Circular Economy Workshops:* Host workshops to introduce circular economy concepts. Explore opportunities to embed circularity in product design, manufacturing processes, and waste management.

7. ESG Integration:

- *ESG Training:* Provide comprehensive training on Environmental, Social, and Governance (ESG) principles. Align business strategies with ESG goals to foster sustainability.

8. Digital Transformation:

- *Technology Integration:* Initiate a digital transformation journey, incorporating technology to enhance efficiency, transparency, and innovation across all business functions.
- *Governance Model Setup:* Establish a Monthly Steering Committee with the CEO as the sponsor. Include a cross-functional team of directors. Appoint an overall Digital Initiatives Lead and an overall Circularity/Sustainability Initiatives Lead. These leads collaborate with digital or sustainability champions representing each function and site.

9. Sustainability Initiatives:

- *Sustainability Projects:* Implement sustainability initiatives such as renewable energy adoption, waste reduction, and eco-friendly packaging. Align these initiatives with Ubuntu Polder Framework goals.

10. Cooperative Business Approach - Build Partnerships: Foster collaborations with stakeholders, suppliers, and competitors to create a cooperative business environment. Emphasize shared value creation and mutual success.

11. Community-Centric Projects - Local Community Engagement: Develop and execute projects that directly impact local communities positively. Prioritize initiatives addressing societal needs and environmental concerns.

12. Continuous Improvement - Feedback Loops: Establish mechanisms for continuous feedback from employees, customers, and stakeholders. Use this input to refine and improve business practices aligned with Ubuntu Polder Framework principles.

13. Performance Metrics and Reporting - Develop Metrics: Define key performance indicators (KPIs) that measure success in terms of societal impact, environmental stewardship, and stakeholder satisfaction. Regularly report progress and achievements.

14. Leadership Communication - Internal and External Communication: Communicate the organization's commitment to the Ubuntu Polder Framework transparently. Share success stories, challenges, and future aspirations with both internal and external audiences.

15. Iterative Adaptation - Adapt to Changing Realities: Remain agile and open to adapting the Ubuntu Polder Framework strategies based on evolving business landscapes, societal needs, and environmental challenges.

By establishing a governance model, including a Monthly Steering Committee and dedicated leads, businesses can ensure sustained commitment and collaboration throughout the Ubuntu Polder Framework implementation process. This structure enables efficient coordination, oversight, and integration of digital and sustainability initiatives across functions and sites.

Here's a simplified diagram representing the roadmap for transitioning from Business as Usual to embracing the Ubuntu Polder Framework, including the governance model:

1. Understanding the Ubuntu Polder Framework approach
2. Educational Initiatives
3. Leadership Alignment
4. Assessment of Current Practices
5. Stakeholder Engagement
6. Circularity Integration
7. ESG Integration
8. Digital Transformation + Governance Setup
9. Sustainability initiatives
10. Cooperative Business Approach
11. Community-Centric Projects
12. Continuous Improvement
13. Metrics and Reporting
14. Leadership Communication
15. Iterative Adaptation

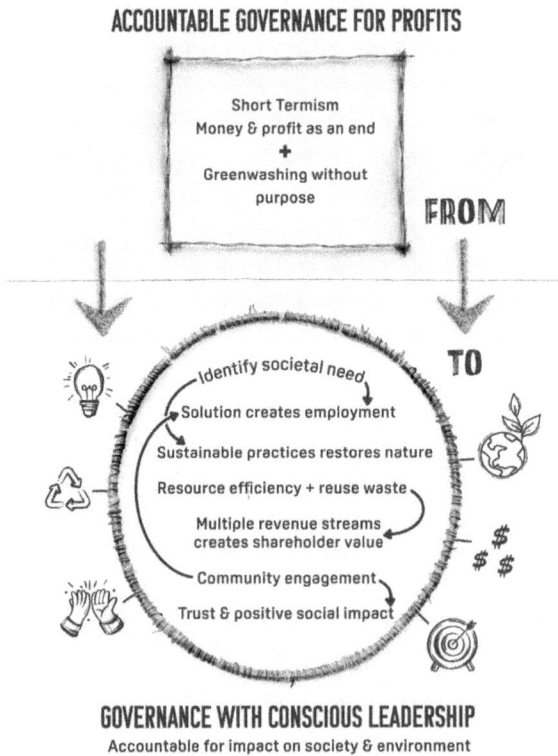

ACCOUNTABLE GOVERNANCE FOR PROFITS

Short Termism
Money & profit as an end
+
Greenwashing without purpose

FROM

TO

Identify societal need
Solution creates employment
Sustainable practices restores nature
Resource efficiency + reuse waste
Multiple revenue streams creates shareholder value
Community engagement
Trust & positive social impact

GOVERNANCE WITH CONSCIOUS LEADERSHIP
Accountable for impact on society & environment

This diagram outlines the sequential steps in the transition process, emphasizing the interconnected nature of each phase. The governance model (8. Digital Transformation + Governance Setup) is a pivotal element to ensure effective coordination and oversight throughout the entire journey.

Implementation - Structuring Holistic Business Transformation - A Comprehensive Approach

The theoretical transforms into the practical as we explore the intricacies of implementing the Ubuntu Polder Framework. This section provides a comprehensive approach, detailing the necessary organizational shifts, cultural adjustments, and leadership recalibrations required for a successful transition. It's a blueprint for leaders ready to embark on the transformative journey of reshaping their business from the core.

In the chapters that follow, we will unpack each element, weaving together theory and application, to empower leaders with the knowledge and tools needed to embrace the Ubuntu Polder Framework and redefine the role of business in our interconnected world.

When embarking on the different transformation journeys I initiated in my career one constant I recognized the importance of establishing a clear governance structure to drive holistic change. This structure was designed to embed digitalization, sustainability, circularity, and ESG at the core of our business model. Here's how we structured the implementation:

1. *Executive Committee Steerco:* At the highest level of our organization, we formed a cross-functional Steerco (Steering Committee) led by the Executive Committee. As the CEO, I took on the role of the overall sponsor. This Steerco was tasked with providing strategic oversight and guidance for the entire transformation journey.

2. *Champion Networks:* To ensure that the transformation had the necessary impact and reach, we established two networks of champions, each focused on specific areas of the transformation:

- Sustainability and Circularity Network: This network was dedicated to driving initiatives related to sustainability and circularity. Its role was to identify, champion, and coordinate projects within their respective functions and sites that aligned with these objectives.
- Digitalization Network: The digitalization network concentrates on harnessing the power of technology to advance our business. They were responsible for exploring and implementing digital solutions and opportunities.

3. *The 80-20 Rule:* We followed the principle that 20 percent of individuals typically drive 80 percent of the change. With this in mind, we carefully selected individuals within the organization who had the potential and passion to be these drivers of change. These champions were identified as the key agents to lead the transformation efforts.

4. *Training and Capacity Building:* Once identified, these champions received comprehensive training to enhance their capabilities. This training was essential to equip them with the skills and knowledge needed to effectively lead the change within their respective functions.

5. *Identifying Key Areas:* The champion networks played a pivotal role in identifying key areas within their functions that required attention and transformation. They served as internal change agents who could spot opportunities and challenges unique to their domains.

6. *External Partnerships:* Recognizing the need for external expertise and collaboration, these champions also coordinated with external partners who could accelerate the transformation efforts. This involved forming alliances with organizations and experts in the fields of sustainability, circularity, and digitalization.

7. *Inspiration and Alignment:* To kickstart the sustainability and circularity initiative, we invited Professor Gunther Pauli to address our top 250 Senior Leaders. His insights and expertise helped inspire our senior leadership and set the tone for the transformation in this domain. Likewise, we brought in digital experts to showcase the possibilities of smartly deploying technology to our leadership, aligning them with the digitalization objectives, and crucially removing the fear of digital and showing them how it could help transform their work to become more fulfilling, more rewarding by removing all aspect of work that are either Dull, Dirty or Dangerous.

8. *Lead/Coordinator for Champion Networks:* Each of the champion networks had a designated lead or coordinator. These individuals were responsible for summarizing the actions taken, tracking progress, and addressing any hurdles faced by the champion teams. They also prepared the agenda for the monthly Steerco meetings, ensuring that progress and challenges were regularly reviewed at the highest level.

By structuring the implementation in this manner, we were able to create a robust framework that not only fostered collaboration and innovation but also ensured that the entire organization was aligned with the holistic business transformation objectives. This approach allowed us to drive change effectively, addressing the challenges and opportunities presented by digitalization, sustainability, circularity, and ESG at the heart of our business framework.

FOUR

APPLICATIONS OF THE UBUNTU POLDER FRAMEWORK: IMPLEMENTING CHANGE

REALIZING CHANGE ACROSS BUSINESS PHASES

R evisiting the Dutch expression "Geen woorden maar daden" – not words but deeds, we embark on a pragmatic journey. In the preceding chapters, we delved into the rationale behind the Ubuntu Polder Framework, explored its foundational pillars, and outlined the overarching framework. Now, our focus shifts from theory to practice as we illuminate the real-world application of this transformative model.

In this section, we will unveil the Ubuntu Polder Framework in action, demonstrated through tangible examples spanning various countries and scenarios, traversing the entire value chain, from the upstream processes to the mid-stream initiatives and onward to the downstream outcomes. Each case study is a testament to the model's adaptability and efficacy, showcasing its ability to foster collaboration, drive sustainable practices, and generate holistic value.

However, I want to briefly share my foundational experiences that shaped my approach to business and leadership.

Embarking on a Global Odyssey: Early Career Ventures and Empowering Experiences

In the rich tapestry of my early years, I embarked on a journey that transcended continents and cultures, molding my worldview. Having finished my high school and before starting my university, a fortuitous detour led me to a two months internship at France Glaces Findus, Nestlé France, setting the stage for a transformative experience in the city of lights.

Paris, with its enchanting streets, became the backdrop of my first foray into the corporate world at the tender age of 18. Nestlé, with its familiar brands and transparent value chain, captivated my imagination. The empowerment I felt, entrusted with implementing changes in a multinational company, fueled my passion.

As I had to complete two internships of six months each as part of my university, I reapplied to Nestlé France and I managed to get an opportunity to work in the sales administration of the Export department. I again was feeling empowered when I was allowed to implement the process improvements I proposed. In my third year of university, my journey moved beyond the borders of the West, when drawn toward the promise of the developing world, I searched for an internship in Asia. Rejections from several Nestlé companies in Asia, citing language barriers, became the catalyst for my resilience. Determined to break through, I enrolled in an intensive Indonesian language and culture course, adding a cultural layer to my pursuit.

The turning point came with a phone call to Denis Chavanis, the Commercial Director of Nestlé Indonesia. Dialogue ensued, a dance of negotiation and commitment. The warmth of personal interaction echoed in his laughter, resonating as he requested my CV once more, as he had thrown away my first CV.

Upon arriving in Jakarta for my internship, our dialogue continued. Denis Chavanis, in a candid moment, asked about my previous earnings at Nestlé France. His response, an offer to double that amount, not only reflected his commitment but fueled my determination. The challenges were met with enthusiasm, working on supply chain issues during the day and marketing projects at night.

The pinnacle of my internship unfolded as I presented recommendations to the Management Committee of Nestlé Indonesia. Proposing the establishment of a Logistics department, my vision was embraced, marking the genesis of a transformative journey. As I returned to university, the advocacy for logistics and supply chain integration bore fruit, symbolizing the impact of individual initiative.

This segment of the journey captures not just the professional milestones but the personal negotiations, laughter, and shared commitment that shaped my early years. From the romantic allure of Paris to the vibrant streets of Jakarta, this chapter sets the stage for the symphony of empowerment, resilience, and the relentless pursuit of growth—a prelude to a career woven with Ubuntu Polder principles.

Upon completing my studies, I embraced the call of international exposure as an expat with Nestlé. The journey commenced at 22, traversing eight countries across three continents. It was in Jakarta that my personal and professional worlds converged as I met my wife and laid the foundation for a global family.

This short section encapsulates the formative years, from the enchanting streets of Paris to the bustling metropolis of Jakarta, shaping a narrative woven with empowerment, resilience, and a relentless pursuit of growth. It sets the stage for a career marked by transformative experiences and a commitment to the principles of the Ubuntu Polder Framework.

INNOVATING UPSTREAM, MIDSTREAM, AND DOWNSTREAM

Brewing Success in the Tropics: From Bali to Hanoi

The moment I stepped off the plane in Indonesia for the first time felt like entering the crocodile section of the Rotterdam Zoo. The curtain of moisture enveloped me, accompanied by the scent of clove cigarettes, reminiscent of my visits to the Indonesian Embassy in The Hague for visa formalities. It was a sensory overload—exotic, new, intense, and utterly captivating.

During my years in Indonesia, the importance of Supply Chain and the essence of holistic optimization became crystal clear. After proposing the setup of a Logistics department at the end of my internship, I found myself not just rejoining but deeply immersing myself in its operations for over two years. My focus extended to order processing, where I revolutionized the administrative approach, shifting from product-centric to customer-centric.

Amidst the challenges and triumphs, my heart oscillated between my passion for Marketing and the emerging love for Supply Chain. The dichotomy surfaced during Friday sessions organized by Nandu Nandkishore, a Group Product Manager, who generously shared his marketing insights. The conflicting sentiments were apparent, but the experiences in Supply Chain became a crucible for my growth.

Transitioning to Sales, the prospect of being stationed in Bali, the dreamy holiday destination, tantalized me. However, fate led me to Surabaya, a vibrant city with its unique challenges. Assigned to revive the Confectionery business, I collaborated closely with Nandu, my mentor, navigating the intricacies of distribution. A bold move into the red-light district yielded thriving sales, a testament to the effectiveness of targeted distribution.

As we ventured into the chocolate business, the tropical climate posed challenges. Establishing a "cool chain" and focusing on strategic distribution points became imperative. Creativity blossomed as I orchestrated mall events, leveraging the burgeoning family-oriented culture. The introduction of a celebrity added a spark, generating media attention and boosting brand awareness.

However, my penchant for interviews without prior approval triggered a swift response from the head office, leading to the introduction of a media (SOP) Standard Operating Procedure. Despite the minor setback, my journey continued, and I was entrusted with the role of Sales Operations Manager, overseeing the entire branch's operations.

The abrupt shift from Surabaya to Jakarta, joining the Sales Marketing Productivity Team (SMPT) project, marked a rapid turn in my expatriate career. The EMAS project, an immersion in marketing, sales, and supply chain optimization, became my hands-on MBA. The success of the project amplified my visibility and set the stage for future endeavors.

In Vietnam, the initial shock of Ho Chi Minh City's airport and the memorable market experiences in Hanoi painted a vivid picture of cultural contrasts. The role of Group Product Manager for Coffee and Beverages marked my foray into Marketing, a domain I had long aspired to embrace.

The coffee landscape in Vietnam was undergoing a miraculous transformation, mirroring the country's ascent as the largest Robusta producer globally. My marketing journey unfolded with challenges, including internal resistance and organizational silos. The shift in leadership brought a more motivated country manager, salvaging the situation and fostering a collaborative environment.

My tenure witnessed the exponential growth of the coffee business. Recognizing the local preference for fresh coffee, I strategically shifted focus to Nescafé 3in1, revolutionizing our approach. Agronomic efforts supported local coffee bean production, reinforcing Nestlé's commitment to sustainable practices.

The subsequent move to the Philippines as Business Executive Officer for Coffee marked a significant chapter. The Philippines, with one of the largest Nestlé coffee businesses globally, presented both an honor and a challenge.

This section of my Ubuntu Polder Journey encapsulates the dynamic interplay between personal aspirations, professional challenges, and the ever-evolving landscape of Southeast Asian markets. From the humid streets of Jakarta to the vibrant markets of Hanoi, each step contributed to my holistic understanding of business and reinforced the Ubuntu Polder principles.

Before delving into the illuminating real examples of the Ubuntu Framework in action, we must briefly introduce two vital elements that underpin the model's practical implementation: Innovation and Technology. These elements are pivotal in shaping the success stories we are about to unveil, acting as catalysts for transformation, and enabling the Ubuntu Polder Framework to manifest its full potential.

Harnessing Innovation: an Ubuntu Polder Framework Approach

This section delves into the dynamic realm of innovation within the context of the Ubuntu Polder Framework. It explores how this model serves as a catalyst for harnessing innovation at its core. By intertwining African wisdom and Dutch ingenuity, we uncover a unique approach that not only embraces technological advancements but also ensures they align with sustainable and equitable principles.

In the spirit of the Ubuntu Polder Framework, "Embrace Innovation" stands as a fundamental pillar with far-reaching implications for individuals, organizations, and societies alike. This commitment to innovation is not confined by geographical borders, cultural distinctions, or corporate hierarchies. Instead, it radiates from every member of the organization, with a simple guide I referred to as the business ABC: "A" for attention to detail, "B" for the courage to escalate issues, and "C" for the unyielding curiosity. Innovation belongs to no specific team or department; it should permeate every facet of the organization.

Encouraging each department to embrace creativity and innovation is akin to unlocking a treasure trove of possibilities. The essence of innovation lies in the power of curiosity and the freedom to pose questions, no matter how unconventional they may seem. It's about creating a culture where innovation becomes a natural byproduct. When teams are empowered to think creatively, they discover ingenious solutions, streamline their processes, and shift their focus to what truly matters.

I consistently challenge every member of the organization to ponder a simple yet profound question: "What if we could revolutionize or solve specific challenges within our department or area of responsibility to enhance our lives and work?" This challenge serves as an open invitation to think expansively and, more importantly, to translate those innovative ideas into tangible actions. In doing so, we transform innovation from a theoretical concept into a practical and impactful force that shapes our collective journey.

Maximizing Technology: an Ubuntu Polder Framework Perspective

Going beyond mere adoption, this section elucidates the Ubuntu Polder Framework's distinctive perspective on maximizing technology. It's not just about using technology for the sake of efficiency; it's about leveraging it as a powerful tool to drive positive societal and environmental impact. Be brave.This exploration sheds light on how the framework navigates the intricate landscape of technological integration while staying true to its foundational principles.

In the contemporary landscape, technology stands as a formidable driving force, but it's essential to differentiate between technology and the realm of social media. While social media platforms often contribute to the widening chasm of polarization by virtue of programmed algorithms that prioritize contentious content, technology encompasses a broader purpose. The root of polarization often lies in the absence of empathy, where entrenched beliefs are perpetuated, reinforcing the conviction that one's viewpoint is unassailable. The emergence of Web 3.0 holds promise in tackling these issues inherited from the era of Web 2.0, fostering more constructive online interactions.

As our world becomes increasingly automated and digitized, computers are becoming increasingly adept at handling tasks that demand precision and calculation. This presents a unique opportunity for humans to redirect their focus toward endeavors that necessitate emotional intelligence and ethical discernment, thus guiding the trajectory of artificial intelligence and technology. The Ubuntu Polder Framework, with its commitment to sustainability, circularity, and the astute use of technology, offers a blueprint for transforming challenges.

My Time in the Philippines: Embracing the Ubuntu Polder Framework

Drawing from personal experiences in the Philippines, this section provides a firsthand account of embracing the Ubuntu Polder Framework in a specific cultural and economic context. It details the nuances of applying the model's principles in a diverse setting, illustrating how cultural sensitivity and adaptability are integral to the successful implementation of transformative change.

In the heart of the Philippines, amidst the enchanting beauty and complex challenges, I had the privilege of applying the principles of the Ubuntu Polder Framework to create a positive impact. The Philippines, like many developing nations, grappled with corruption, poverty, and severe income inequality. Its history bore the scars of political unrest and uprisings, yet it was a place where resilience and happiness prevailed. As I assumed full P&L accountability for the Coffee Business, I felt the weight of revitalizing a declining yet profitable venture. But this was more than a business challenge; it was an immersion into the interconnected lives of our extended value chain.

"Team, let's leave the confines of our offices, don muddy boots, and step into the tropical landscapes of the Philippines," I declared to my team. Together, we traversed the sun-drenched coffee plantations, engaging in the labor-intensive, ant-bitten process of harvesting ripe coffee cherries. This hands-on experience embodied the Ubuntu Polder Framework's commitment to understanding the realities on the ground.

Our journey unfolded, weaving through buying collection centers and coffee factory, witnessing the alchemy from roasting to instant coffee creation. We explored local coffee shops, decoding the "coffee vibe" and immersing ourselves in the language of menus and consumer behavior.

But our mission was more profound than merely boosting profits. It was about empowering local coffee farmers, whose livelihoods were threatened by the influx of Vietnamese beans. The Philippines, historically a coffee giant, faced a crisis. To revive Nescafé, we launched the Coffee and Health campaign, not just as a marketing strategy but as a catalyst for positive change.

"Increase radio communications at the buying stations, inform farmers of global prices," I instructed, aiming to cut out middlemen and ensure fair earnings for farmers. We introduced "model farmers" to set examples, implementing sustainable practices like intercropping and organic fertilization.

As Nescafé celebrated its 70th anniversary, we didn't just mark the occasion; we published a book, *Kapihan*, a testament to our journey and a communication arsenal for our PR campaign. Simultaneously, the Coffee 101 training course was born, ensuring our knowledge wasn't confined to our organization but accessible to all.

Recognizing our responsibility as ecosystem leaders in the coffee industry in the Philippines, we sought to transcend conventional business boundaries. It was in this spirit that the idea of establishing a local chapter of the Sustainable Agriculture Initiative (SAI) took root.

The Sustainable Agriculture Initiative, based in Brussels, had laid down global guidelines for sustainable agriculture, including the Common Code for Coffee (CCCE). Nestlé, as a founding member, had been a key participant in these initiatives. However, the challenge was to bring these global guidelines to the local context in the Philippines.

The vision was clear—to create a platform where industry players could collaboratively adapt and translate the global SAI guidelines, ensuring they resonated with the unique conditions and challenges faced by Filipino coffee farmers.

A call was sent out to the key stakeholders in the local coffee industry. Representatives from various segments—from farmers and agronomists to processors and distributors—gathered with a shared purpose. The initial meetings were a symphony of diverse voices, each contributing their insights on how to localize the global guidelines effectively.

As we delved into the discussions, it became apparent that the adaptation process required a deep understanding of the intricate web of challenges faced by our local farmers. The lush landscapes of the Philippines, while picturesque, hid the complexities of a sector struggling with issues like fluctuating global prices, traditional farming practices, and the impact of climate change.

The journey to localize SAI guidelines was not without its hurdles. It demanded a delicate balance between maintaining the integrity of the global standards and tailoring them to address the specific needs of Filipino coffee farmers. The discussions sometimes grew intense, reflecting the passion and commitment of each participant to contribute meaningfully to the initiative.

Gradually, consensus emerged, and a framework began to take shape. The local chapter would not be a mere replication of global standards; it would be a dynamic entity, capable of evolving alongside the ever-changing landscape of Philippine agriculture.

The process of adaptation involved translating the guidelines into actionable plans. This meant creating a roadmap that considered the realities on the ground—from the types of coffee grown to the challenges faced by farmers during harvesting and processing.

To ensure the sustainability of the initiative, we aimed to foster collaboration beyond our corporate walls. Inviting NGOs, government bodies, and even academic institutions into the conversation enriched the dialogue and broadened the scope of our collective impact.

Finally, the SAI local chapter in the Philippines was officially established. It stood as a testament to the commitment of the industry to sustainable practices and marked a significant milestone in our journey toward holistic business transformation.

The impact of this local chapter extended beyond our borders. The adaptations made in the Philippines resonated with SAI communities globally, reinforcing the notion that sustainability is not a one-size-fits-all concept. Through this initiative, we not only elevated the practices within our country but contributed to a global conversation on the importance of tailoring sustainability measures to local contexts.

As the inaugural meetings concluded, there was a palpable sense of achievement and unity among the participants. The SAI local chapter in the Philippines became a beacon of hope, symbolizing the power of collaboration and adaptability in fostering sustainable agriculture and transforming the coffee industry from within.

In the rapidly evolving digital landscape of 2006, we embraced online presence, navigating platforms like Friendster and foreseeing the potential of Facebook in its early stages in Asia. A Digital Champion, Jason Avanca, played a pivotal role in expanding our online footprint, eventually joining the Global Digital Acceleration team.

My journey in the Philippines was not just about business; it was a narrative of positive change, community upliftment, and knowledge sharing. The Ubuntu Polder Framework found its true expression in this tropical haven, proving that a holistic approach could bring about lasting and positive change in both business and society.

Elements of the Ubuntu Polder Framework leveraged:

Cultural Sensitivity and Adaptability:
The narrative emphasizes the importance of understanding the unique cultural and economic context of the Philippines. This aligns with the Ubuntu Polder Framework's principle of embracing diversity and adapting to different settings.

Interconnectedness and Extended Value Chain:
The journey involves a commitment to understanding the perspectives of those on the ground, particularly the coffee farmers. This hands-on experience exemplifies the Ubuntu Polder Framework's emphasis on interconnectedness and recognizing the value chain beyond traditional business boundaries.

Sustainable and Circular Approach:
The transformation goes beyond boosting profits; it focuses on implementing a sustainable, circular approach to business. This aligns with the Ubuntu Polder Framework's core principles of embedding sustainability at the heart of the business model.

Community Engagement and Empowerment:
The section highlights the initiative to immerse the team in the lives of coffee farmers, elevating the local coffee industry. This approach echoes the Ubuntu Polder Framework's commitment to creating value for stakeholders and fostering positive change within communities.

Educational Initiatives and Knowledge Sharing:
The emphasis on training courses, knowledge dissemination, and the Coffee 101 experiential training course reflects the Ubuntu Polder Framework's commitment to education and sharing knowledge for the benefit of all stakeholders.

Environmental Stewardship:
The promotion of sustainable practices in coffee farming, such as intercropping, pruning, and organic fertilization, aligns with the Ubuntu Polder Framework's focus on environmental stewardship and responsible business practices.

Industry Leadership and Collaboration:
Recognizing their role as industry leaders, the initiative to establish a local chapter of the Sustainable Agriculture Initiative (SAI) demonstrates the Ubuntu Polder Framework's principle of cooperation and understanding the interconnectedness of the global community.

Celebrating Milestones and Positive Impact:
The celebration of Nescafé's 70th anniversary and the publication of a book demonstrate the Ubuntu Polder Framework's recognition of milestones and the opportunity to spread positive messages and pride within the local coffee industry.

Digital Innovation and Adaptation:
The strategic decision to explore new platforms, including Facebook, showcases the Ubuntu Polder Framework's adaptive nature and recognition of the importance of staying at the forefront of digital innovation.

Switzerland: Navigating Global Complexity

My professional journey led me to Switzerland, a country renowned for its breathtaking landscapes and precision. While the train rides from Geneva to Vevey painted picturesque scenes of blue lakes, snow-capped Alps, and hillside vineyards, my focus shifted to the intricacies of managing a global organization at Nestlé's head office.

Tasked with overseeing the Developed Markets in the Coffee SBU (Strategic Business Unit), I delved into the complexity of running a multinational corporation. In this role, I faced the challenges of driving a common agenda for coordinated change across diverse markets. The experience revealed the intricacies of a global organization, emphasizing the need for a more cohesive approach to brand communication.

Heading the Communication portfolio, I spearheaded the update of a brand communication framework, aiming for a more coordinated and coherent brand presentation globally. However, organizational changes brought forth a new Head of SBUs, known for his discerning standards. The rollout of new brand visual designs was halted, despite positive testing across countries. This experience underscored the delicate balance required in navigating organizational shifts and maintaining a unified brand strategy.

A pivotal moment occurred during a visit to Japan, where my proposed recommendations for a brand turnaround were met with resistance from the new Head of SBUs. Despite advocating for a collaborative approach, I found myself in a challenging position. This encounter highlighted the importance of fostering an open, transparent atmosphere to drive innovation and constructive dialogue.

While Switzerland presented its own set of challenges, my time in the SBU witnessed significant achievements, including the global rollout of the Nescafé plan and Coffee & Health initiatives. Collaborating on the European rollout of 3in1 and creating a Nescafé 75-year celebratory book added noteworthy chapters to the journey.

Despite the achievements, a desire to return to the dynamic developing world markets lingered. Expressing this to Nestlé leadership, I ultimately found an opportunity as the Managing Director of the Tropical Cluster in central Africa, reinforcing my commitment to contributing to positive change in emerging markets.

My Time in Central Africa: Transforming Road Safety and Tackling Malaria in Cameroon

In the heart of Central Africa, my time in Cameroon became a vibrant canvas for the Ubuntu Polder Framework's transformative impact on road safety and the anti-Malaria efforts. The "Safe Way, Right Way" and "Anti-Malaria" Initiatives emerged as a beacon, illuminating the potential for holistic business transformation to extend beyond corporate confines and touch the lives of communities.

Our family's exploration of Cameroon was a kaleidoscope of experiences, defying my preconceived notions of arid Africa with lush greenery and year-round rain. A remarkable 1000 KM road trip unfolded, weaving through the tropical South to the desertic North. As we traversed the diverse landscapes, the Kingdom of Bafut welcomed me with the honor of being crowned Prince, a recognition of our company's commitment to community building.

In the midst of this diverse and vibrant setting, the Tropical Cluster, comprising Cameroon and neighboring countries, functioned as a collection of loosely connected individual operations. Determined to bring coherence to this diversity, we embarked on the transformational journey of unifying these operations under the theme "On est Ensemble" – "we are together/we are one." Overcoming language barriers, tribal differences, and economic disparages, we achieved alignment, resulting in both business and community development success.

At the core of our endeavors was the establishment of the "Safe Way, Right Way" Foundation, a collaborative initiative dedicated to addressing the pressing issue of road safety in the region. Together with Total, Brasseries du Cameroun, and other partners, we recognized the need for a pre-competitive effort to improve road safety.

The "Safe Way, Right Way" Foundation exemplified the Ubuntu Polder Framework's principles, drawing strength from collaboration, community-centricity, and collective responsibility. In a continent and world where road safety posed a critical concern, the initiative showcased the power of businesses uniting to address societal issues.

In the context of Africa's alarming road safety statistics, with daily fatalities and injuries, the "Safe Way, Right Way" initiative took a pioneering step. Worldwide, 1.3 million people die on the roads annually, with Africa bearing 20% of these accidents despite having only 2% of the global car park. In Cameroon, where road accidents were particularly deadly, the initiative aimed to make a meaningful impact.

The Ubuntu Polder Framework's core principles were woven into the fabric of the initiative:

Collaboration and Interconnectivity: The "Safe Way, Right Way" Foundation epitomized collaboration by uniting corporations and partners in a pre-competitive effort. The company actively engaged in addressing road safety, recognizing the shared responsibility for the well-being of the community and the workforce.

Community-Centric Approach: Aligned with the Ubuntu Polder Framework, the initiative prioritized community development by directly contributing to the well-being and safety of local communities. The broader impact of road safety on the population, beyond employees, underscored its significance as a community development effort.

Collective Responsibility: Acknowledging the shared responsibility for road safety, Nestlé, as a responsible corporate citizen, joined hands with other industry players. The initiative addressed the interconnectedness of road safety with business factors such as absenteeism, productivity, and brand image.

Anti-Malaria Initiative: Within our operations, the number one cause of absenteeism was malaria. While there is no vaccine to prevent malaria, even without it is relatively straightforward to avoid the conditions that put individuals at risk of a malaria-infected mosquito bite. In 2013, the Anti-Malaria campaign was initiated, introducing a checklist for employees to follow and implementing a buddy system for mutual accountability. Participating employees who adhered to the checklist received rewards such as mosquito repellent and nets. This approach not only significantly reduced absenteeism due to malaria but also turned participating families into model households, inspiring neighbors to adopt preventative measures.

The "Safe Way, Right Way" initiative and the Anti-Malaria campaign exemplify commitment to positive societal impact in Cameroon and beyond. The Ubuntu Polder Framework found expression in a transformative experience, showcasing the profound influence of collaboration, community-centricity, and collective responsibility in addressing critical societal challenges. As our family's journey in Cameroon came to an end, the next chapter awaited me as the CEO of Nestlé Pakistan, marking the continuation of a purpose-driven professional odyssey.

My Time in Pakistan - Empowering Deep Rural Communities - the Deep Rural Initiative

Venturing into the landscapes of Pakistan, my family and I embarked on a transformative journey, uncovering the Ubuntu Polder Framework's profound impact on deep rural communities. At the heart of this section lies the story of the Deep Rural Initiative, a testament to sustainable development and the framework's adaptability to diverse socio-economic realities.

The commitment to make a positive impact on the lives of those in deep rural Pakistan led to the initiation of the "Deep Rural" project. The persistent challenge of reaching rural areas due to the substantial cost of "last mile" delivery prompted innovative solutions. Leveraging our existing milk collection network, which routinely visited villages for milk collection, we transformed these trips into opportunities for product distribution. Our simple insight was that we already had our milk containers go to these villages to collect the milk, so instead of going there empty and coming back with the milk, we engineered to add a box on the truck to load the relevant products and bring them to our milk collection centers.

We equipped our collection agents with training in warehousing operations, product knowledge, and sales skills. Now they could utilize the time between milk collections to distribute our products to village shops. Simultaneously, we empowered unemployed women in these areas through specialized training in nutrition, hygiene, and product knowledge. These women became agents of change, hosting information sessions for housewives and offering product samples. Village events for sampling and branding further strengthened our presence. Through this initiative, we bridged the last mile gap while conducting activations for affordable and nutritious products.

In semi-rural regions, a parallel program unfolded to stimulate employment opportunities and enhance product distribution. Collaborating with the Benazir Income Support Programme (BISP), a government initiative empowering women through unconditional cash transfers, we identified women eager to engage in gainful employment.

Comprehensive training in nutrition, hygiene, selling techniques, and product knowledge paved the way for these women to receive an interest-free loan in the form of Nestlé products. Through diligent efforts, they not only repaid their loans but also established sustainable businesses, gaining a renewed sense of self-worth and pride.

The Collaboration with Akhuwat Pakistan, the largest interest-free microfinance program, extended microloans to women aspiring to scale their businesses. Over 2,000 rural Pakistani women embarked on their journeys into the retail business, marking a significant stride towards economic empowerment and greater financial inclusion.

As a CEO in Pakistan, my family and I embraced the country with open hearts, exploring its diverse provinces and immersing ourselves in the rich culture. Despite security protocols, I traversed every province, connecting with teams and distributors, understanding local issues, and motivating everyone.

The weekends offered opportunities to explore the city of old Lahore, its narrow streets teeming with life, vibrant colors, and inviting tastes. From visiting mosques and bathhouses to ending the day on a restaurant rooftop overlooking the Badshahi mosque, each experience was a testament to the richness of Pakistani culture.

Our holidays in Hunza, nestled in the Himalayas, provided a unique blend of breathtaking landscapes, distinct food, and a captivating culture. This interest in local culture, food, and people allowed me to connect the dots between different countries and share the positive aspects of these seemingly misunderstood places on Facebook.

During my tenure as CEO, we undertook transformative projects, such as the paperless and cashless value chain project. Recognizing the complexities of the manual payment system for milk collection, we partnered with TELENOR to introduce a mobile payment system. This not only streamlined operations but also transformed the lives of illiterate farmers, providing them with a daily record of income and facilitating access to mobile loans. We had to lobby the Central Bank, who had to pass some legislation to open the way for our system to proceed, but it was a real win-win-win solution. We got rid of the heavy administration, the mobile company opened a whole new value stream, but what excites me the most is the life-transforming impact it had on our farmers. Many of them were illiterate and lived often up to a few hours walking from the nearest bank.

Therefore, many didn't even have a bank account and when in need of money, like for example the wedding of their child, they had no other option but to go to the local loan sharks, who would charge exorbitant rates. Many farmers had loans they took years to repay. All this changed as, with the introduction of this mobile payment system, they now had a daily record of income from a reputable source. This allowed them to quickly build up a good credit rating and put them in a position to be able to apply for a mobile loan on-line, from the comfort of their home, at the normal interest rates.

The Deep Rural Initiative and other community-building endeavors were part of Nestlé's commitment to being a responsible corporate citizen. Water preservation initiatives, including certification with WWF and collaboration with farmers for precision agriculture, further demonstrated our dedication to addressing global issues.

The commitment to sustainable practices extends to water conservation, and one noteworthy initiative is the implementation of Alliance for Water Stewardship (AWS) across its global operations. This initiative is designed to enhance water efficiency, reduce consumption, and contribute to the responsible use of this vital resource.

Nestlé has been at the forefront of environmental sustainability, and the AWS certification, achieved in collaboration with the World Wildlife Fund (WWF), is a testament to this commitment. The AWS standard is a comprehensive framework that evaluates the responsible use of water within a company's operations. It not only assesses internal water management but also considers external influences, such as community and watershed impacts. Nestlé Pakistan was the first Nestlé market in the world to achieve AWS certification.

The AWS certification goes beyond traditional water management practices. It considers the entire water cycle, from sourcing to consumption and discharge, taking into account the social, economic, and environmental dimensions of water usage. Nestlé's participation in this program demonstrates a holistic approach to water stewardship that aligns with the principles of the Ubuntu Polder Framework.

To achieve AWS certification, The company has implemented various water-saving technologies and practices across its facilities. These may include:

1. Water Recovery and Recycling Technology:

- Installation of advanced water recovery, treatment, and recycling technologies in factories.
- The technology enables the reuse and recycling of water from dairy operations, contributing to overall water conservation efforts.

2. Precision Agriculture and Drip Irrigation:

- Collaborating with farmers to promote precision agriculture and the adoption of drip irrigation.
- Precision agriculture involves using technology to optimize crop yields while minimizing water usage, contributing to sustainable farming practices.

3. Community Engagement and Education:

- Engaging with local communities to raise awareness about water conservation.
- Implementing educational programs to promote responsible water use and empower communities to actively participate in water preservation.

By obtaining AWS certification, Nestlé demonstrates not only a commitment to responsible water management within its operations but also a recognition of the interconnectedness of water resources with the broader environment and communities. This initiative aligns with the Ubuntu Polder Framework's emphasis on collaboration, community-centric approaches, and collective responsibility.

Obtaining AWS certification is not a one-time accomplishment but an ongoing commitment to continuous improvement. The company must remain dedicated to refining its water management practices, exploring innovative technologies, and actively participating in global efforts to address water scarcity and promote sustainable water use.

In summary, AWS water-saving initiatives reflect a comprehensive and collaborative approach to water stewardship, aligning with the principles of the Ubuntu Polder Framework and contributing to positive environmental and societal impacts.

Elements of the Ubuntu Polder Framework Leveraged:

Inclusivity and Empowerment: The Deep Rural Initiative epitomizes the Ubuntu Polder Framework's emphasis on inclusivity and empowerment. By providing training and opportunities to women in deep rural areas, Nestlé actively promoted their economic inclusion, thus addressing a critical societal need.

Collaborative Efforts: The collaboration with government programs like BISP and Akhuwat Pakistan aligns with the Ubuntu Polder Framework's spirit of collaboration. As responsible corporate citizens, organizations joined hands to drive positive change and empower women in deep rural regions.

Community-Centric Approach: The Ubuntu Polder Framework places a strong emphasis on community development, and the Deep Rural Initiative directly contributes to the betterment of rural communities by creating employment opportunities and improving access to nutritious products.
Nestlé's Deep Rural Initiative demonstrates the power of collaborative efforts, inclusivity, and a community-centric approach in driving positive change in deep rural Pakistan. This transformative project aligns perfectly with the Ubuntu Polder Framework's core principles, making a substantial impact on the lives of women and their communities, while also fostering economic empowerment and financial inclusion.
The journey in Pakistan was not just about professional accom-

plishments but also about embracing the beauty of the country, building connections, and fostering positive change in deep rural communities. As the next challenge beckoned—a merger project for East Africa and Southern Africa—I approached it with the same courage and perseverance that defined our efforts in Pakistan. The Ubuntu Polder Framework continued to guide my leadership style, reinforcing the belief that positive impact is possible through collaborative efforts and a community-centric approach.

My Time in East and Southern Africa

This section serves as a comprehensive reflection on experiences in East and Southern Africa. It weaves together the threads of diverse initiatives, showcasing the framework's adaptability and efficacy across different regional landscapes. From the bustling urban centers to the serene rural expanses, the Ubuntu Polder Framework's impact resonates, proving its applicability as a transformative force on a broader scale.

These sections collectively paint a vivid picture of the Ubuntu Polder Framework in action, providing tangible examples of how it transcends theory to become a powerful driver of positive change in various contexts around the world.

Africa is often portrayed as one homogenous entity, but the continent's diversity is awe-inspiring. From the southern tip in South Africa to the eastern edge in the Horn of Africa, the landscapes, cultures, and cuisines shift dramatically. It's a place where every weekend and holiday offers an opportunity for adventure, whether it's a safari, a hike, a deep dive into history, or simply a visit to a spa or restaurant.

In my role, I embarked on the ambitious mission of merging the East African Cluster with the Southern African Cluster. This journey was more than just a corporate restructuring; it was a deep dive into the intricate dynamics of the region.

The Right Mindset and Cultivating the Buy-in: Unlocking Potential in ESAR (East and Southern African Region)

We immediately focused on creating the foundations that would enable the company to unleash its potential in ESAR. In May 2018, we established an ESAR Integration team to ensure a seamless transition and integration process that wouldn't disrupt our relationships with customers and consumers. Right from the outset, our approach was to unite everyone in ESAR around the opportunity.

Our journey involved co-creating a forward-looking approach to build our Dream Region, placing people at the core, forming One Solid Team with a shared vision and a strong sense of purpose and togetherness. The latter half of 2018 was dedicated to crystallizing our ESAR plans, clarifying our vision for this Dream Region, and outlining the concrete actions required to achieve our objectives.

Balancing the focus and attention between South Africa, the "big brother," and the "smaller countries" posed another significant challenge. I often referred to a Dutch expression: "wie het kleine niet eert, is het grote niet weerd," which means those who don't honor the small are not worthy of the big. South Africa's unique history, with its isolation during apartheid, led to differences in economies, wage structures, and trade patterns compared to other ESAR countries.

In the past, logistical challenges and the presence of ten landlocked countries in ESAR had resulted in higher consumer prices. Our operational setup struggled to maintain a steady supply of goods across the region. We realized that our locations in rural South Africa were plagued with failing infrastructure and governance issues.

These challenges necessitated a Popular Positioned Products (PPP) strategy, where long-term thinking and immediate action were required. My team and I immediately began laying the foundation for sustainable, profitable growth in this region.

Addressing Nutritional Challenges

As we delved into the local diets of ESAR, we discovered a prevalence of affordable but nutritionally inadequate "tummy fillers." Pap, a cornmeal made from milled white maize, was a staple. It could be prepared as sweet porridge or stiff starch, often accompanied by a sauce.

Studies revealed a staggering 729% overconsumption of starch compared to a healthy reference diet in sub-Saharan Africa (SSA). This diet led to micronutrient deficiencies, particularly among children under five. Tragically, children in sub-Saharan Africa were over 14 times more likely to die before the age of five than their counterparts in developed regions. This trend extended into adulthood, with alarming rates of overweight and obesity in countries like South Africa.

A nourishing, sustainable food system was imperative for the region's well-being, but healthy food was not universally available, affordable, or appealing. Nutritional quality was pivotal to addressing malnutrition, and Nestlé had a clear role to play. While delivering over 15 million fortified servings per day through its portfolio was significant, we believed we could do better. Notably, South Africa had taken steps to address its health challenges, introducing a sugar tax in 2019 and a sodium limit in 2021.

In the context in East and Southern Africa which was rich with diversity, challenges, and opportunities, the importance of the communities was immediately clear to me. They needed to be resilient and develop independently, instead of waiting for a central government to come to the rescue. This insight was setting the stage for the RE2AL initiative's transformative journey.

RE2AL: Transforming Lives and Businesses through Ubuntu

Embarking on the RE2AL (Realizing Empowered and Enabled African Livelihoods) initiative in South Africa marked a pivotal chapter in my journey, a testament to the transformative power of the Ubuntu Polder Framework.

The roots of the RE2AL initiative were deeply embedded in a partnership that transcended conventional business objectives. Nestlé forged an alliance with the Makhoba Trust, a community with a history deeply intertwined with the challenges of Apartheid, and Inyosi Empowerment. While the Makhoba community had reclaimed their ancestral lands, the need for more—infrastructure, opportunities, and a sustainable future—persisted. The Ubuntu Polder Framework became our guiding philosophy, emphasizing cooperation, interconnectedness, and a commitment to sustainable development.

At the heart of the initiative was a dedication to empower the youth and women of the Makhoba community. This went beyond economic empowerment; it was about offering the youth a chance to shape their destinies. Agri-preneurship training and dairy farm internships were provided, aligning with the Ubuntu Polder Framework's emphasis on skill development and community involvement.

The partnership between the Makhoba Trust, Nestlé, and Inyosi was more than a business collaboration—it was a living example of the Ubuntu Polder Framework. Our goal was not just to meet immediate business objectives but to create a thriving ecosystem. The vision extended beyond the local context; we aimed to connect the Makhoba community with the wider world, fostering sustainable relationships.

The impact was profound and multifaceted. The Makhoba Trust evolved into more than a dairy supplier; it became a symbol of hope for the community. The initiative encompassed a crèche for working mothers, a vegetable-growing initiative, vocational training, and a vibrant, high-functioning commercial dairy. Systematic tracking of impact, from budgets to training, mirrored the principles of the Ubuntu Polder Framework, creating value, fostering cooperation, and acknowledging the interconnectedness of the world.

In our pursuit of sustainability, we implemented innovative solutions. Leveraging Nestlé's R&D expertise, we transformed Black wattle, the most widespread invasive alien tree, into a fodder mix for cows. Similar to the moringa initiative, this not only provided nutritious feed for the cows but also contributed to reducing methane emissions. Other initiatives included replacing artificial fertilizers with chicken dung, intercropping different grass types for efficient water retention, and integrating water sensors for precise irrigation. All these efforts transformed the farm into a Net Zero Carbon emission dairy farm, while also increasing the yield per cow.

The RE2AL initiative stands as a testament to the Ubuntu Polder Framework's efficacy in collaboration, sustainability, and community empowerment. It is a blueprint for the future, not just for Nestlé but for all stakeholders. This framework emphasizes ecosystems, partnerships, and a profound commitment to creating a better, more sustainable world.

As I reflect on this transformative journey, the Ubuntu spirit emerges as more than a concept—it's a living reality. RE2AL is not just an individual case; it's a precedent-setting example of how businesses can be a force for good. The Ubuntu Polder Framework finds its true expression in RE2AL, inspiring others to follow in these impactful footsteps and showcasing the potential for businesses to transform lives, businesses, and the environment through the power of Ubuntu.

Empowering Sub-Saharan African Youth: SSA Youth Alliance

One of the pressing challenges worldwide, especially in developing countries, is youth unemployment. With over 71 million young people unemployed globally and more than 500 million underemployed or in precarious jobs, the need to equip the youth for a rapidly changing job market is evident. Traditional education often falls short in preparing them for the evolving world of work. Over 60% of children starting primary school today are projected to work in jobs that do not yet exist, requiring the right skills and experience to navigate this shifting economic landscape.

Recognizing that the youth are the future leaders, Nestlé launched a global Youth Campaign. The goal was to prepare young people to enter the workforce as inspiring leaders, successful entrepreneurs, and game-changers, regardless of their field or level of expertise. This initiative aimed to build thriving, resilient, inclusive, and peaceful communities, aligning with the UN Sustainable Development Goals.

From South Africa, we took the initiative to establish the "Sub-Saharan Regional Alliance for YOUth." This alliance comprised organizations deeply committed to addressing the critical issue of youth unemployment, particularly prevalent in Sub-Saharan Africa, where over 70% of the population is below 30 years old. This region houses 20% of the global youth population, and it's projected to double by 2055. Shockingly, 70% of working youth continue to grapple with extreme or moderate poverty.

In Sub-Saharan Africa, 65% of youth face unstable employment, unemployment, or job searching. This challenging scenario called for collaborative efforts from corporations across the East and Southern African Region (ESAR) to enhance job employability and job creation. Nestlé, along with like-minded organizations such as Adcorp, Publicis, NielsenIQ, ABB, and Microsoft, joined hands to create this powerful alliance. Their shared passion revolved around helping young people acquire the skills necessary to thrive in the world of work.

The alliance embarked on several initiatives, implementing employability programs, mentorship, and training initiatives to equip the youth with essential workplace skills. One flagship event each year was the "CEO & Youth Connect," where young participants had the opportunity for a Q&A session with the CEOs of the seven participating partner organizations. These CEOs committed to mentoring young individuals, forging lasting connections, and providing invaluable guidance.

The Sub-Saharan African Youth Alliance has made significant strides, focusing on employment and employability. To date, the alliance has reached over 20 million individuals through various media platforms and has empowered more than 50,000 youth through workshops. These workshops included CV clinics, career coaching, and mentorship programs led by the CEOs of the alliance's partner organizations.

The use of social media played a pivotal role in expanding the alliance's reach to even more youth across Sub-Saharan Africa. As the alliance continues to drive its plans, the aim is to expand partnerships in Central West Africa and align its brands with a clear sense of purpose.

The ultimate goal is to expand the alliance, engage additional like-minded partners, establish a stronger presence in other countries, and persist in the noble mission of empowering the youth. In doing so, the Sub-Saharan Regional Alliance for YOUth exemplifies the Ubuntu Polder Framework in action, emphasizing cooperation, interconnectedness, and a shared commitment to creating opportunities for young people in the region.

Project Hatcher: Transforming Business through Expanding the Ecosystem

In a rapidly evolving business landscape, adaptability is paramount. The journey from merely selling branded products to monetizing branded experiences often demands the integration of technology and service layers—a shift that many corporate marketing teams are ill-equipped to handle. While recognizing the need for this transformation, achieving real traction in implementing it can be a significant challenge.

As we ushered in 2022, the imperative of future-proofing our business became non-negotiable. With the practicality of upskilling an already busy marketing team in mind, I decided to look beyond our organization and tap into our ecosystem to source the required skills and expertise.

In the East and Southern Africa region, we are accomplishing this through the Hatcher Platform, an initiative that exemplifies the Ubuntu Polder Framework by creating a thriving ecosystem. This platform seamlessly connects our innovation network, harnessing our agility and expertise to extend our solutions beyond the core, thus enhancing the resilience of our business.

The Hatcher Platform serves as a conduit for collaboration with local innovators to address region-specific challenges. By enabling local-for-local open innovation, it empowers us to collaborate with external partners, incubate innovative concepts, and transition from selling branded products to selling immersive brand experiences. This strategic shift aims to introduce additional revenue streams and enhance the margins for our brands.

Our active pursuit of external partnerships enables us to access complementary skills for testing, learning, and forming strategic alliances. In some cases, these alliances even involve equity shareholding, enabling us to acquire capabilities that were previously beyond our reach. We are also open to exploring M&A

opportunities that can further enhance our ability to delight consumers.

Within the Hatcher program, we send project briefs to entrepreneurs across the East and Southern Africa region. The response has been nothing short of remarkable, with hundreds of pitches pouring in from 11 countries within the region. These proposals are diligently evaluated, and the winning teams are granted a modest budget and access to our organization to transform their ideas into reality.

To bridge the gap between these entrepreneurial talents and our marketing teams, we enlisted the support of COOi studios, a dynamic group of young innovators led by Sandiso Sibisi. COOi studios serves as an innovation acceleration partner, specializing in delivering innovation initiatives that aim for exponential growth. They apply design thinking techniques, embrace digital technologies, and cultivate a culture of innovative thinking within organizations.

Project Hatcher embodies the Ubuntu Polder Framework by fostering collaboration, interconnectivity, and a shared commitment to ushering in a new era of business. It's a testament to the power of ecosystems, where diverse talents converge to transform challenges into opportunities and embrace the ever-evolving landscape of business with resilience and ingenuity.

Project Blue

In a groundbreaking collaboration with ECCO2, Nestlé initiated a project at our Food and Creamers manufacturing factory in South Africa, marking a significant stride towards sustainability and circularity. ECCO2's proprietary technology, designed for industrial-scale carbon capture and utilization, was at the core of this innovative venture.

The project's focal point was the capture and utilization of carbon dioxide emissions from the factory boiler house. Through ECCO2's cutting-edge technology, these emissions were transformed into food-grade baking soda, specifically sodium bicarbonate. This strategic move not only addressed environmental concerns by reducing carbon emissions but also created a valuable resource with diverse applications.

The ripple effect of this initiative extended to the biscuit manufacturing process, notably impacting the production of our beloved KitKat product. By incorporating the locally produced food-grade baking soda, we achieved a seamless circularity within our manufacturing ecosystem. This not only showcased our commitment to sustainable practices but also generated additional revenue streams through the optimization of resources.

The Project Blue initiative illustrates the Ubuntu Polder Framework's dedication to pushing the boundaries of innovation and sustainability. It stands as a testament to our pursuit of holistic business transformation, embedding circularity, and maximizing the value we derive from our operations. This initiative, like others detailed in this narrative, underscores the belief that businesses can be a force for good, contributing positively to the environment while fostering economic growth and innovation.

In the everyday ritual of sipping our daily cup of coffee, we unknowingly contribute to a staggering amount of waste—99.8 percent of the coffee bean goes unused. The discarded peel, a treasure trove of antioxidants, and the spent grounds post-brewing are often cast aside without realizing their potential. It's a narrative that doesn't add up. When a mere 0.2 percent of the coffee bean is utilized, there lies an opportunity to do 500 times better—a chance to not only spur economic growth but also address the needs of communities.

Nestlé, in collaboration with Ekofungi Limited and The Future of Hope Foundation, has embarked on a visionary pilot project named Project Indigo: Mushrooms. This initiative ingeniously transforms the waste by-product of coffee production, the spent coffee grounds, into a valuable resource by cultivating mushrooms. The result is a circular economy model that not only minimizes waste but also generates multiple avenues for positive impact.

The pilot project has set the stage for an experimental oyster mushroom farm in Harare. Beyond its immediate goal of scaling tangible results, this farm serves as a training center, empowering women from the community to cultivate and harvest mushrooms. The harvested mushrooms become a source of livelihood for these women, addressing both economic needs and contributing to community sustenance. Notably, the mushrooms find a second life in another MAGGI product, showcasing the potential for a holistic approach to resource utilization.

The circularity of this initiative doesn't stop there. Following mushroom cultivation, the residual "soil" proves to be a valuable component as chicken feed, introducing yet another revenue stream into the equation. This holistic and sustainable model exemplifies commitment to pushing the boundaries of innovation, embracing circularity, and demonstrating the transformative power of conscious business practices.

Project Indigo: Mushrooms is not just about reducing waste; it's a testament to the belief that businesses can be a force for good, creating value at every stage of the process while contributing positively to the environment and communities.

Unlocking Zimbabwe's Business Transformation and the ZiWeb Initiative

Nestlé Zimbabwe, an integral part of the East and Southern Africa Region (ESAR), has played a pivotal role in the organization's journey to adapt and transform. Established in August 2018 as part of Nestlé's reorganization in Sub-Saharan Africa, Nestlé Zimbabwe stands as the second-largest country where the company has been doing business for approximately six decades, and Nestlé Zimbabwe has nurtured a thriving factory with a dedicated workforce and beloved brands such as Nestlé Cerevita, Nestlé EveryDay, and Nestlé Cremona.

Upon my first visit to Zimbabwe, a startling reality came to light —our products were priced nearly half compared to our competitors. At Nestlé, quality is a non-negotiable standard, and we fortify our products to ensure nutritional superiority. Consequently, our products are often priced at a premium compared to competitors. It was, therefore, a surprise to find our products sold at a significant discount.

While we were selling products in the local currency, producing them in Zimbabwe required importing most of our raw and packaging materials using FOREX. The official exchange rate was pegged at 1 Zim Dollar = 1 US Dollar, but obtaining FOREX officially was a daunting challenge. It was only "freely" available on the parallel black market, where the rate was 1 US Dollar = 1.8 Zim Dollars and rapidly deteriorating. Committed to adhering to local rules and legislation, we did not have access to the black market. This situation led to us repeatedly seeking FOREX loans from our head office, loans that we couldn't foreseeably repay. It became evident that our current business model was unsustainable.

Amid these challenges, Nestlé Zimbabwe embarked on a journey of comprehensive transformation, demonstrating the Ubuntu Polder Framework elements.

Elements of the Ubuntu Polder Framework Leveraged:

Collaboration and Interconnectivity: We engaged with local suppliers to shift from a high FOREX intensity model to one that primarily used locally available ingredients for product recipes. Substantial local supplier development was crucial to meet international standards.

Talent Development: On the HR strategy front, we increased the recruitment of local talent in Zimbabwe for key positions, including the factory manager, finance manager, and cluster manager. This not only enhanced our local presence but also contributed to employment opportunities.

Market Sensitivity: We established a team to closely monitor market prices of our competitors, adjusting our pricing more frequently to remain competitive and meet the local market's needs.

Financial Optimization: We optimized our financial assets by assisting employees with Zim Dollar packages, purchasing transport vans for factory workers, and securing long-term media deals with upfront payments, among other strategies. This financial agility was crucial for sustainability.

Today, Nestlé Zimbabwe has a sustainable business model, characterized by organic growth based on real volume growth and the ability to self-generate FOREX for all payments and royalties.

To ensure our team's focus on boosting local production, we allowed customers in Zimbabwe to purchase directly from South Africa for the range we didn't produce. We expanded our production capacity and maximized export opportunities to generate our own FOREX.

From a sales perspective, we significantly broadened our distribution model in traditional and informal trade through distributors and introduced the ZiWeb program, which empowers Zimbabwean women in business to facilitate neighborhood distribution, especially as the primary currency used remains USD.

The efforts of Nestlé Zimbabwe have not gone unnoticed, as the team has received four prestigious awards. These accolades include the Farmer Support Award of the decade, Buy Zimbabwe Insignia Award of the decade, the first runner-up award for the Product of the decade for NESTLÉ CEREVITA, and the first runner-up for the Quality Award of the decade.

In my role as CEO in in East and Southern Africa, I've had the privilege to engage with various stakeholders, including ambassadors, government leaders, business leaders, and civil society leaders, to address socio economic challenges common to the continent. These challenges encompass health issues, including obesity, micronutrient deficiencies, and undernutrition. To combat these challenges, we must collectively focus on affordable food nutrition, promote good healthcare, and encourage wellness, necessitating sustained cooperation and partnerships.

This collective effort demands continuous and long-term commitment, which Nestlé, as the world's largest food and beverage company, is well-equipped to provide. With over 2,000 brands and a presence in 191 countries worldwide, it plays a significant role in addressing these challenges and fostering sustainable growth.

Nestlé's unwavering commitment to Zimbabwe has greatly contributed to the company's credibility when engaging with various stakeholders on the ground. This resilience and dedication to stay through thick and thin exemplify the Ubuntu Polder Framework's principles of interconnectedness and collaboration, contributing to Zimbabwe's transformation and growth.

They furthermore aim to change/nudge consumer behaviors. We focus on reducing food waste and waste reclaiming initiatives. In the RE-Imagine Tomorrow pilot project, we collaborate with Kudoti—a waste recycling tech startup and Destination Green—a buy back centre and have started a pilot for the community of Mqantsa in Tembisa. This project is aimed at empowering 100 waste reclaimers.

I trust that the examples shared throughout this chapter have illustrated the capacity of major corporations to offer products and services that align with societal interests, creating value not only for shareholders but for society at large. The aim is to play a role in poverty alleviation, job creation, and nature restoration. The initiatives presented are intended to contribute to reestablishing communities and nature on their evolutionary trajectories.

While I recognize that I do not possess all the answers and acknowledge that there is still a long way to go, it remains crucial to sustain a spirit of continuous discovery and exploration. I encourage anyone with intriguing ideas to experiment and try out these ideas. Similar to an unwavering commitment to achieving zero accidents in the factories and warehouses, the environmental aspirations demand nothing less than a target of zero harm. Mere 'green' initiatives fall short; the 'reduce, reuse, recycle' mantra, while commendable, does not suffice to halt destruction. The true objective transcends zero, and must strive for regeneration. This entails actively working towards the restoration of ecosystems, encompassing social and economic communities in the process.

In the pursuit of providing consumers with high-quality products and services, our business approach must evolve beyond emission reduction and avoiding harm to the planet. We must shift towards actively doing significant good. The ongoing commitment is to nurture communities, enhance livelihoods, and prioritize the well-being of people. Simultaneously, we must safeguard, renew, and restore natural ecosystems. It is imperative for industry leaders to promote a regenerative approach at a scale that can make a substantial impact.

Ultimately, the goal is to transition from being less harmful to actively doing no harm, progressing towards repairing, replenishing, and building the capacity for regeneration. This vision encapsulates an unwavering commitment to creating a business model that not only sustains but actively contributes to the betterment of society and the environment.

FIVE

CONSCIOUS LEADERSHIP
MANIFESTO

TIMELESS PRINCIPLES FOR LEADERSHIP

n this part of the book I want to talk more about the skills needed for a conscious leader to make transformative changes in his team and or organization. It is in a way a manifesto for conscious leadership; we delve into the profound principles of the Ubuntu Polder Framework that serve as guiding beacons for the new breed of leaders. These principles encapsulate trust, a relentless pursuit of learning, embracing change, networking.

I will then share my personal model/philosophy.

Conscious Leadership: Timeless and Adaptive

This section delves into the core principles of conscious leadership, emphasizing its timeless relevance while adapting to the dynamic landscape of transformative business. It explores how leaders can embody a conscious mindset, aligning with the Ubuntu Polder Framework's ethos to foster ethical practices, inclusivity, and sustainable decision-making. By intertwining timeless leadership values with adaptive strategies, this manifesto sets the stage for a new era of conscientious business leadership.

OVERCOME FEAR OF FAILURE

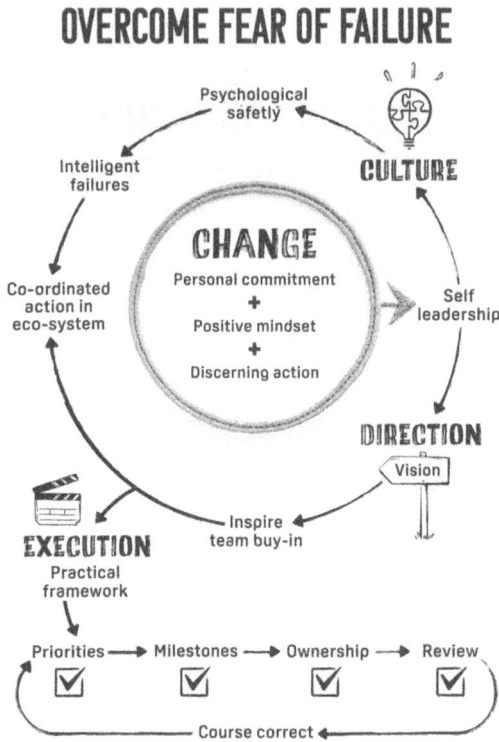

Leadership transcends generations. Conscious leaders recognize that they must adapt to the ever-changing business landscape while staying rooted in timeless principles. The best leaders lead in the present, learn from the past, and strive for a better future. They maintain a broad perspective by staying connected, being the guiding light, and upholding trust, active listening, empathy, and psychological safety as the constants in their dynamic leadership journey.

Conscious leadership, anchored in the Ubuntu Polder Framework principles, embodies a profound commitment to trust, transparency, authenticity, quality, and lifelong learning. These leaders are the beacons guiding us through the dynamic world of business, fostering an environment of unity, growth, and unwavering trust, where every individual's voice is valued, and the pursuit of excellence is relentless.

Soft Skills are Hard Skills

In the journey of life, soft skills often prove to be the hardest and most valuable skills one can possess. These essential attributes— humbleness, kindfulness, and vulnerability—are more than just interpersonal qualities; they are the pillars of conscious leadership and personal growth.

As Rudyard Kipling wisely noted, "When you can meet with Triumph and Disaster, and treat those two imposters just the same," he highlighted the ability to maintain equanimity in the face of success and failure. It's a reminder that humbleness is not the absence of self-confidence but the presence of self-awareness. It's understanding that the world is vast, complex, and ever-changing, and no matter how much we know, there is always more to learn.

Similarly, Socrates' wisdom echoes through the ages, reminding us that the more we know, the more we realize the vastness of our ignorance. This acknowledgment that our minds can never fully grasp the intricacies of the world is the cornerstone of kindfulness. It involves approaching life with an open heart and a willingness to learn from others, recognizing that every individual brings a unique perspective to the table.

A visit to the Apartheid Museum in Johannesburg provides profound insights into the lives of iconic leaders like Nelson Mandela and Desmond Tutu. What strikes a chord in these exhibitions is the profound humbleness that both leaders exhibited. Their motivation wasn't driven by ego or the desire for fame; it was rooted in a genuine wish to enhance the lives of all South

Africans. They exemplified leaders who worked tirelessly for the betterment of society, gaining the unwavering trust of their people.

Nelson Mandela, in particular, stands as a paragon of Level 5 leadership, according to Jim Collins. He epitomized conscious leadership, always working for the greater good rather than personal glory. His charisma, authenticity, and distinctive style, wearing colorful Batik clothing, set him apart as a remarkable leader who was unafraid to be himself. He demonstrated that leadership isn't about being the hero but about dedicating one's energy and wisdom to the greater good.

Another embodiment of humbleness and conscious leadership is Syed Babar Ali in Pakistan. He built his companies during Pakistan's formative years and then partnered with the world's best multinationals, continuing to invest in various initiatives. Beyond business, his commitment to high-quality education led to the establishment of a university that, even after 50 years, maintains its success. His involvement in environmental conservation, as a founder and the 2nd president of WWF, demonstrates a holistic approach to leadership. His ability to connect with presidents, kings, and queens while remaining exceptionally humble is a testament to the power of true humility.

Humble leaders who create enduring, positive change practice gratitude, journaling, exercise, meditation, and random acts of kindness. Their authenticity and dedication to societal improvement make them natural innovators.

The wisdom of the Dalai Lama resonates, emphasizing the importance of combining compassion with intelligence for a happy life. Similarly, Charlie Chaplin's words remind us that we often overthink while under-feeling. Our actions should stem from our hearts as well as our minds.

As a conscious leader, in your life and career you might find that the outward kindness is occasionally misunderstood. It happened to me several times and while I stand firm on my principles, including humility and kindness, I understand the importance of acting appropriately when someone goes against those principles. In these situations I am not afraid to make tough decisions when they are for the right reasons, always doing so in a humane manner. I recognize that "how" I execute decisions is just as crucial as "what" I decide. Vulnerability, as suggested by Brené Brown, is essential, but it must be balanced with the need for leaders to convey confidence and inspiration, especially during challenging times.

The concept of "fake it till you make it" comes to mind, illustrating the delicate line between maintaining confidence and embracing vulnerability. Harvard professor Chris Argyris's Ladder of Inference is a useful framework, emphasizing the importance of building a hopeful narrative based on selected data, assumptions, and conclusions. It's about shaping the story that inspires belief and hope, enabling teams and organizations to take necessary actions.

Connection, gratitude, mindful communication, empathy, and purpose play pivotal roles in my leadership philosophy. Forgiveness is another cornerstone, allowing for personal growth and relationship building.

On the subject of Karma, I believe it's not an external mystical force but an internal reflection. By doing good in the world, you generate a sense of inner well-being. Your actions create reactions within yourself, impacting your self-image and how you are perceived by others. A conscious leader understands that to love others, you must first love yourself genuinely. The intention to always do the right thing aligns with the belief that your reflections in the mirror each morning should be devoid of self-judgment.

In my life, I've internalized Benjamin Franklin's advice that "by failing to prepare, you are preparing to fail." I've also embraced Victor Borge's wisdom that "laughter is the shortest distance between two people." This has guided my ability to connect with others. When words and actions conflict, we should heed Ralph Waldo Emerson's counsel, relying on the language of non-verbal cues.

A holistic view of leadership encompasses these core principles, highlighting the significance of humbleness, kindfulness, and vulnerability in forging genuine connections and making a positive impact on the world.

Trust as the Cornerstone of Leadership

Conscious leaders embody trust as a foundational element of their leadership approach. They understand that trust is the lifeblood of their connection with their teams. Trusting employees to deliver their best, especially in the evolving landscape of hybrid work models, yields remarkable productivity. Leaders also recognize that meritocracy, not favoritism, should be the bedrock of trust, ensuring an inclusive and harmonious team.

Active Listening and Synergy

Active listening is a cornerstone of conscious leadership. Leaders not only lead but actively listen across all organizational levels, fostering an environment where every individual's contribution is valued. Hierarchy, while necessary for accountability, does not diminish the importance of any role. Effective leadership involves influencing minds, providing guidance, and maintaining motivation, particularly in challenging times. Leaders offer optimism, recognizing its significance during adversity.

Transparency and Authenticity

Conscious leaders prioritize transparent, open communication. Sharing the company's state, vision, mission, and values instills a sense of belonging among employees. They acknowledge and celebrate their team's progress, reaffirming the significance of their work. Authenticity, love, loyalty, and empathy are integral to leadership. "Love-driven Leadership" recognizes individual talents, unlocks potential, and fosters loyalty and mutual support within teams.

Psychological Safety and Quality Over Quantity

Leaders create an environment where team members feel safe to point out blind spots and voice their concerns. They embrace diversity and foster a culture where everyone feels valued and free to express their thoughts. Quality over quantity is the mantra, and leaders prioritize curiosity, delving deep into situations, asking questions, and exploring various perspectives. Mistakes are acknowledged, and the "PLUS-DELTA" tool (later in the book on page 118, more on this tool) is used to learn and grow, nurturing psychological safety.

Diversity and Women Empowerment

When my journey in the corporate world led me to Pakistan, I took it upon myself to champion gender balance. This endeavor took shape within Nestlé and through the OICCI (Overseas Investors Chamber of Commerce and Industry) association. OICCI represents nearly 200 companies from 35 countries, spanning 14 sectors of the Pakistani economy, with a collective asset value of over 85 billion USD. Working alongside teams from various companies in my working group, we devised a systematic approach to assess a company's stance on gender balance and chart a clear path toward achieving it. This roadmap prioritized actions and drew from the progressive practices of companies already leading the way. The idea was not to reinvent the wheel but to take inspiration from those who had already made meaningful strides. To encourage further progress, we established an annual prize to recognize the company that demonstrated the most significant advancement.

In 2017, as Vice President of OICCI and Chairman of the CSR committee, I aimed to address gender balance in the corporate landscape of Pakistan with a practical approach. Instead of merely highlighting the need for gender balance and presenting disheartening statistics, I believed that we needed tangible actions to guide organizations. The case for change was understood, and there was substantial buy-in. The issue lay in feeling overwhelmed by the magnitude of the challenge and not knowing where to begin. I organized an OICCI event on this topic and delivered a personal speech to launch the initiative.

I shared a personal story from the 1950s in Paris, where my grandmother was nominated for an award recognizing working mothers. She had raised seven children alone after her husband's early death from tuberculosis. This legacy continued with my mother, who worked throughout her life while raising children, and it extended to me as well. I, too, moved abroad, married, and my wife, like the women before her, decided to work while navigating the challenges of frequent international relocations. This lineage of working women was intertwined with my own career, and it seemed like destiny for me to be involved in promoting women's empowerment.

I then introduced the story of Momina, a young woman who aspired to build a marketing career in a multinational company. However, after becoming a mother and facing societal pressures and personal challenges, she left her job. Her journey mirrored the struggles of many women in Pakistan. Despite her past achievements, she felt that returning to corporate life was impossible. But, encouraged by her family and ex-colleagues, she decided to reapply for a position and was rehired as the administrative assistant to the CEO. The company offered flexible working hours, day-care services, pick and drop support, and her manager and colleagues were sensitive to her needs. Gradually, she regained her confidence, took on more responsibilities, and excelled in her role. Her success story became an inspiration.

The issues of women empowerment, gender balance, and diversity are frequently discussed today. However, the question is whether Pakistani society truly cares about these matters. As CEOs of foreign companies, many care deeply. Yet, it is my belief that the broader society still needs to prioritize these issues. Pakistan ranked 2nd lowest globally for 'Economic Participation and Opportunity for Women' in the World Economic Forum's Gender Gap Report 2014, with only Afghanistan ranking worse. Gender balance is a complex issue in Pakistan, with cultural, stereotype, empowerment, and mental barriers hindering progress. Our first OICCI survey on Gender Balance revealed that most companies have less than 15% women in their workforce, and they struggle to make the necessary changes.

So, why should we care about empowering women to work? The answers include economic growth, social progress, and gender equality. Notably, a 2016 IMF paper estimated that closing gender gaps in economic participation could boost Pakistan's GDP by up to 30 percent.

As OICCI, it made perfect sense for us to take action. When I proposed making women empowerment our joint initiative as Chairman of the OICCI CSR committee, I received unanimous support. While we all agree on the importance of this cause, implementing a women-friendly work environment remains a challenge. Practical issues, such as childcare, safety for working women, and career progression after having children, must be addressed. The OICCI Women initiative aims to offer a concrete path forward, providing a systematic guide for creating women-friendly workplaces. We encourage everyone to join this initiative, as it is vital to transform our companies and society as a whole.

The CSR Committee formulated a 5-step roadmap, complete with real examples of policies, practices, and training for each step. This roadmap focuses on making a visible executive commitment, setting the foundation, enabling female employees to balance work and home, maximizing the potential of female talent, and influencing the world beyond the companies themselves. To track the progress, we also proposed a simple self-assessment scorecard mechanism, enabling organizations to assess their journey from inactive to best practice.

OICCI is responsible for collecting 30% of Pakistan's tax revenues, making their companies influential economically and socially. By working together to empower women, it can create a substantial impact on our society and the wider business community. We aimed to start a movement in Pakistan, in Asia, and even globally. Most of OICCI companies operate in multiple countries, and by promoting this pragmatic approach, can make a meaningful difference.

Pakistani women have immense talent, and it's time to unlock their potential for a brighter future. This initiative is not about celebrating a few famous women; it's about nurturing the brilliance of the women already working in the organizations and making them role models for others. In Nestlé Pakistan, we have a program called Kero Aitemaad (Let's trust each other) where we share stories and experiences of women in the workforce with female university students, breaking stereotypes and instilling hope, ambition, and self-confidence.

This is the impact it wants to amplify.

Unlocking the Flow State: Flow, the state of selflessness where time becomes abstract, is essential for peak performance and innovation. Understanding the moments in your life when you experienced flow can guide your efforts to access this state at will.

Achieving Individual and Group Flow: Recognizing the conditions that lead to individual flow is valuable, whether it's through thrilling adventures or moments of freedom. As a leader, fostering group flow within your team involves finding the delicate balance between challenge and skill. It's the zone of breakthroughs and innovation, made possible by trust, psychological safety, and a leader's positive energy.

Building Trust: Trust is the cornerstone of effective cooperation within the Ubuntu Polder Framework. Credibility, reliability, empathy, and motivations all contribute to trust. It's a formula that underpins collaboration and progress, essential for making the model a reality.

Relentless pursuit of learning: Conscious leaders believe in continuous learning and growth. They emphasize the importance of being present in every step of the journey, appreciating the beauty of life, and remaining curious. This innate curiosity and passion drive leaders to embrace five methods of learning: formal education, reading, active listening, focused observation, and experimentation, acquiring new skills, and self-reflection. Leaders understand that curiosity, passion, and experimentation are the driving forces behind learning by doing, propelling them to new heights of leadership.

Education

While I often criticize the education system, my point is that it's a relic of the industrial age, designed for the production and management of physical goods. Today, we need a shift from goods to experiences and from repeating the same to innovative approaches. It's easy to critique the system, but improving it is a complex challenge.

The Montessori system offered an alternative, but it may not work for all children, as it requires self-motivation and discipline. Most kids today are easily distracted, especially by smartphones and computers, choosing the path of least resistance.

I believe education should help individuals discover their purpose, moving beyond mere money-making. Business schools often focus on making money rather than solving problems. Therefore, in addition to the core hard skills like language, math, biology, and physics, education must foster soft skills like emotional intelligence, observation, reflection, and creative thinking.

In a rapidly changing world, many traditional hard skills can become redundant, with computers, powered by AI apps, bots and "agents," capable of handling them. Alvin Toffler's advice resonates: Prepare children to learn, unlearn, and relearn. The main goal of education should be to teach how to adapt and thrive in an ever-evolving landscape.

LEARNING, TRUST, AND EMBRACING CHANGE

The Power of Reading: Leaders are Readers

In the words of Rebecca Solnit, "A book is a heart that only beats in the chest of another." Books have the power to connect us to the hearts and minds of authors, providing insights and wisdom that can shape our understanding of the world.

Curating Knowledge: I've always been an avid reader, passionate about books and eager to explore new ideas that ignite my mind. When I discover a topic that fascinates me, I transition into my "spreading the news" mode, sharing these revelations with others. Many people may not share the same enthusiasm for reading, so I've developed the skill of summarizing complex concepts and delivering them in easily digestible formats—a crucial ability for any business leader. This skill has enabled me to absorb complexity and distill it into its essential elements, simplifying the story.

Learning by Doing: My approach to learning involves swiftly moving from understanding the current state to envisioning a better future. I believe in the power of small, consistent, incremental improvements. This philosophy compels me to embark on small projects, experiment, fine-tune them, and eventually scale them. As you saw in the previous parts of the book, this approach has been consistently applied in my career.

Storytelling and Engagement: Reading books has taught me the art of storytelling and the importance of avoiding monotony. Engaging books build tension, then release it, and rebuild to a climax. These elements are essential for any leader when delivering speeches and presentations.

Witnessing the Big Picture: Reading trains the mind to see the big picture. In a book, information is unveiled gradually, and characters and events may initially appear unrelated. As a reader, you must retain these details and assemble them into a coherent narrative. This fosters the skill of constructing scenarios and anticipating what comes next.

Patience and Persistence: Reading also imparts patience and persistence. It's unlikely that you'll finish many books in a single sitting, so you must cultivate a reading routine as a healthy habit.

Maria Popova's insights underscore how books help us understand people, the world, and ourselves. They act as a telescope into the minds of others, revealing the starry expanse of our own consciousness. Literature is a tool for living with more wisdom, goodness, and sanity. It simulates reality, enabling us to learn from others and become global citizens. It makes us more empathetic by exposing us to diverse perspectives and the consequences of various actions.

Books provide solace from loneliness, expressing emotions more honestly than real-life conversations. They offer maps to our inner selves, helping us navigate our emotions and thoughts.

Moreover, books prepare us for failure. In literature, failures are often treated with compassion and understanding.

Reading puts us in a state of flow, forcing us to stay in the present moment and command our brains to focus.

The object we call a book is not just a physical entity but a reservoir of potential, like a musical score or a seed, awaiting its transformation in the hands of a reader.

Focused Observation and Experimentation: Unveiling Life's Laws

As the sage Nisargadatta reminds us, "Love tells me I'm everything, wisdom tells me I'm nothing, and in between these two banks flows the river of life." This river of life carries a valuable lesson in focused observation and experimentation, a technique I wholeheartedly embrace in my pursuit of knowledge and understanding.

Life's Principles: Through focused observation and experimentation, we uncover Life's Principles—immutable rules that, like the laws of physics, govern various aspects of existence. These principles extend to domains as diverse as religion, sports, and business. To illustrate, consider the act of prayer or fasting in Islam, the precision needed to sink a golf ball into the hole, or the commitment essential for a business leader to make sound decisions. These scenarios share a common thread: commitment.

Conquering Fear: The human mind often amplifies potential pitfalls, leading to procrastination or half-hearted efforts. This self-doubt can become a self-fulfilling prophecy, sabotaging our endeavors. Yet, understanding this Life Law allows us to harness its power. By directing our focus toward the desired outcome, we increase the likelihood of realizing it. Overthinking and fear of failure, especially when fatigued, can hinder progress.

The Tortoise's Wisdom: It's important to remember that many paths lead to success, and the shortest road isn't always the best. Recall the tale of the tortoise and the hare. The tortoise prevailed because it began its journey without hesitation and persevered till the finish line. Starting is often more significant than fretting about the perfect path.

The Power of a Calm Mind: My experiences in Jiu Jitsu and golf have reinforced the significance of maintaining a calm mind. A tranquil, present, and self-aware state allows us to correct our course before errors become irreversible. In this state, we learn and grow with purpose. We feel in control and less over-whelmed, fostering the courage to seek guidance when necessary.

Discovering the World's Patterns: With understanding comes the ability to discern patterns in the world, akin to the revelations in the movie *The Matrix*. This doesn't imply that we should strive for machine-like perfection; rather, we appreciate the beauty of perfect imperfections, such as in art. Imperfections stir emotions and give us goosebumps.

Embracing Imperfections: Just as we relish the uniqueness of art, we should celebrate life's imperfections. This notion is exempli-fied in the contrast between Indonesian Batik and Printed Batik. It's in the unpolished, the flaws, the missing pieces that emotions are kindled.

Future Challenges: In the future, we'll need to engage in system-level strategic thinking and prioritize effective problem-solving. To address complex challenges, we must harness uniquely human values, fostering innovation and creativity. Contextual and creative knowledge, along with a deeper understanding of our humanity, are essential. The process of collective learning and inspiration from diverse fields will drive progress.

The Art of Experimentation: The ability to experiment, adapt, and make mistakes is crucial. Just as Steven Colbert emphasizes the need for "image-ination," we learn by trying, failing, and getting up. In the pursuit of ambitious goals, course corrections are as vital as the initial trajectory. The rocket to the moon was only on course 2% of the time; the rest was off-course, much like a journey.

Learning from New Skills: Learning transcends theory and extends into the application. One such example is photography. I've always enjoyed it, but immersing myself in the art of manual photography elevated my passion. A photography trip to the Masai Mara and a course in 2021 marked a turning point.

Progress and Enjoyment: Learning new skills may be challenging, but the steepest progress occurs early on, providing boundless energy and enjoyment. Theory is essential, but I believe in swiftly applying new knowledge. Learning in a beautiful setting enhances receptivity, and immediate application cements learning.

Curiosity and Beyond: Hobbies like photography stimulate curiosity, a skill indispensable in our professional lives. Photography is more than just capturing images; it encourages anticipation, pattern recognition, patience, and perspective. Different people capture the same events in unique ways, emphasizing the importance of diverse viewpoints.

The Scientific Benefits of Learning: Learning isn't merely a personal pursuit but also has scientific benefits. Positivity fuels learning, with dopamine driving our quest for knowledge. Happiness is a precursor to success, and achieving a state of happiness in the present yields better results.

Knowledge Multiplication: Flux of knowledge depends on attention and time. To maximize the benefits of learning, passion is paramount. Individual knowledge of A and B surpasses collective knowledge of A and B separately, emphasizing the value of collaboration and knowledge sharing.

Reflection: A Paradigm Shift

The world is changing, and our approaches to work, communication, expression, information, and entertainment must evolve. A shift from a zero-sum game mentality to one of abundance is imperative. Knowledge is boundless, and it multiplies when shared.

This comprehensive approach to learning encompasses both personal and professional growth, fostering adaptability, creativity, and a deeper understanding of the world. Embracing the interconnectedness of knowledge and wisdom, it is a journey toward a better future.

Self-Reflection: The Heart of Learning

As outlined in my learning model, the journey of learning comprises several interconnected elements: theory (acquired through education and reading) coupled with an inner drive of curiosity and passion motivates us to practice (experiment, observe, and actively listen). Subsequently, we evaluate and reflect, perpetuating a cycle of continuous growth. This iterative process leads to fine-tuning, evolution, and the adjustment of our theories. Ultimately, we master these concepts and integrate them into our broader life experiences.

The Challenge of Reflecting: In my experience, the most challenging aspect of this journey is the art of reflection. In a world where constant activity and social media leave us little time for introspection, reflection has taken a back seat. Shortened attention spans perpetuate this issue, and, as a result, we often turn to others to solve our problems.

The Importance of Reflection: Reflection is essential to our learning model. Just as consciousness is vital in leadership, reflection is the key to our personal and professional growth. It's the bridge that connects theory and practice, allowing us to fine-tune our understanding and skills.

The PLUS-DELTA Tool: To facilitate systematic and regular reflection in both my personal and business life, I employ the PLUS-DELTA tool. It's a simple yet effective technique that can be applied on an individual level or within an organization for team reflection. To use this tool, divide a page with a line, labeling the left side "PLUS" and the right side "DELTA." On the PLUS side, record what you're content with, what you've excelled in. On the DELTA side, jot down what didn't go as planned, where improvements are needed, and how to initiate those changes.

Focused Reflection: The PLUS-DELTA tool is most effective when focused on specific topics or areas over several reflection sessions, rather than shifting topics every week. Dedicate a few hours of uninterrupted reflection time, scheduled in your calendar. Reflecting on past PLUS-DELTA entries helps you identify patterns and assess areas that need attention.

Application in Management Meetings: I've introduced this tool in my management meetings to gauge team feelings about various topics. It's a quick process, taking only five minutes, and it ensures transparent, anonymous feedback for all participants. By implementing suggested changes based on this feedback, the team feels heard and is more open to providing constructive input.

Outside-In Perspective and Networking: As we transition from a world focused on material production to a knowledge-based society aided by AI and robotics, continuous learning is paramount. The only way to stay relevant in this shifting landscape is to adopt a lifelong learning approach. Alvin Toffler's prediction that the illiterate of the 21st century will be those who can't learn, unlearn, and relearn is more relevant than ever.

The Challenge of Embracing Change: Bill Clinton, in his inauguration speech, posed a poignant question that remains relevant today: Can we make change our ally rather than our adversary? It's a question that echoes through history and continues to resonate in our lives.

Breaking Free from Comfort Zones: Marina Cuesta reminds us that to attain something we've never had, we must be willing to undertake actions we've never taken before. In this journey, choosing the path of uncomfortable growth over comfortable stagnation is key. Reflect on areas in your life or work where comfort may be holding you back and contemplate what discomfort is required for growth.

The Ideal Start-Up Team: Dave McClure's wisdom emphasizes the importance of assembling a diverse start-up team, consisting of hipsters, hackers, and hustlers. Each member brings a unique perspective: hipsters focus on aesthetics, hackers on functionality, and hustlers on execution. The lean start-up approach, centered on rapid launches and validated learning, highlights the significance of agility and adaptability.

The Perils of Resisting Change: Throughout history, we've been reminded that change is the only constant. Yet, resistance to change persists in society, organizations, and individuals. In business, inertia often leads to counterproductive reactions during challenging times. Instead of focusing on customer satisfaction and innovation, cost-cutting and inefficient tactics are employed. This resistance can be detrimental.

Embracing Uncertainty: A healthier approach to change is to acknowledge that all times are uncertain times. The pace of change may be rapid, but it's equally true that the future remains unpredictable. Life isn't black and white; often, there are no clear rights or wrongs, and multiple scenarios are possible. In our VUCA (Volatile, Uncertain, Complex, Ambiguous) world, we must understand that the answers aren't always straightforward, and change takes time to yield results. Patience and tolerance are essential virtues.

The Imperative of Change: Stagnation is often the prelude to decline. The Dutch proverb "Hoogmoed komt voor de val" (arrogance comes before the fall) serves as a stark reminder. We are at a critical juncture where we must embrace change as a collective belief and initiate a dialogue about what a better future could look like. Common vision leads to change and progress.

Managing Change with a Calm Mind: To make change less intimidating, maintaining a calm and focused mindset is essential. When making decisions, it's often better to decide and course-correct than to remain indecisive. Taking responsibility for your beliefs and actions is empowering, as is focusing on the fundamental principles of life and creating a harmonious execution.

Navigating the Challenges of Change: Two significant biases pose challenges during change. The Experience Bias arises when past experiences are no longer relevant due to evolving circumstances. The Availability Bias underscores the need to double-check plans when answers come too easily. Both biases require vigilance during the change process.

The Power of Belief and Persistence

Challenges and resistance have a peculiar way of fueling determination. In the face of naysayers, holding steadfast to your beliefs can propel you forward. Be resolute, take responsibility for your thoughts and actions, and focus on the journey rather than the destination.

Embracing Change

In a world of constant transformation, embracing change and fostering an environment of trust, innovation, and cooperation is the path to a brighter future. Remember that change is not the enemy; it's an opportunity for growth, development, and lasting impact.

Sense Making: The Power of Clarity

Simplicity and Minimalism: In the realm of communication, George Bernard Shaw's words remind us that the assumption of effective communication can often be an illusion. True communication requires clarity and understanding, transcending mere words.

The Art of Simplicity: "Nothing to do, nowhere to go." These words by Mark Nepo resonate deeply. The acceptance of the present moment grants the power to accomplish anything and explore every possibility. It's a call for simplicity and mindfulness, which allows us to embrace life fully.

Wisdom from Visionaries:

- Leonardo da Vinci's timeless wisdom echoes the essence of simplicity as the ultimate sophistication.
- Albert Einstein's advice emphasizes making things as simple as possible without oversimplifying.
- E. F. Schumacher draws the line between complexity and genius, highlighting the courage needed to simplify.
- Charles Mingus reveals the creativity in simplifying the complicated.
- Joshua Reynolds strikes the balance between too little and too much, underscoring the importance of exact simplicity.
- Colin Powell recognizes great leaders as skilled simplifiers who offer solutions everyone can understand.

The Quest for Clarity: Francois Gauthier underscores that clarity is more crucial than certainty. In a world where change is constant, clarity allows us to navigate uncertainty effectively.

Evolution from Scarcity to Abundance: Throughout history, humanity has transitioned from a world of scarcity to one of abundance. The industrial revolution led to a profusion of goods, changing our perception of scarcity. In the 21st century, we've entered an era of experience where we seek fulfillment in intangible and meaningful aspects of life. Paradoxically, this abundance of choice can lead to anxiety, creating a 'white noise' of options.

Desire vs. Love: A provocative statement suggests that desire may hold more importance in relationships than love. Love is a biological need, while desire is driven by motivation and ambition. This concept extends to material possessions, where the desire to own often surpasses the satisfaction of ownership.

The Idea of Simplifying Life and Owning Less to Reduce Clutter and Achieve Mental Clarity: Accumulating less and letting go of unnecessary possessions can lead to a more peaceful and focused life.

Photography and Empathy: Photography is described as an exercise in simplifying complex landscapes into simple stories. It also teaches a vital lesson about empathy. The challenge of keeping people's interest in one's photos is a reflection of our inherent self-focus. To connect with others' emotions and stories, empathy is essential.

Contrast Leads to Clarity: The power of contrast in achieving clarity is highlighted. By understanding what you don't want, you can clarify your desires and find purpose and direction in your life.

Self-Care and Positivity

The importance of curating what you expose yourself to is emphasized in self-care. Constant negativity can lead to increased stress and weakened immunity. Actively seeking out positivity and good influences, even in difficult times, is a powerful form of self-care.

Words and Sense Making: In times of crisis, effective leaders provide a clear path to the future. By painting an attractive and vivid picture of the destination, leaders inspire and motivate their followers. This sense-making process is a catalyst for action and dialogue which, in turn, drives progress.

Global Challenges and Polarization: However, the modern world faces a scarcity of effective leaders who can make sense and inspire. The lack of robust debates on critical issues and the challenges of geopolitics and polarization further complicate matters.

The Role of the Ubuntu Polder Framework: The Ubuntu Polder Framework can provide a structure for embracing simplicity and clarity in the business world and beyond. By emphasizing empathy, clarity, and effective leadership, it can guide organizations and societies toward constructive change. In a complex and changing world, the Ubuntu Polder Framework can be a beacon of simplicity and clarity, enabling positive transformations.

NETWORKING, PERSONALIZED GROWTH, BREAKING ROUTINES

Making Connections: YPO and Networking

The concept of building a network can often seem overwhelming, but it simply boils down to having many interactions. These interactions can take various forms, from unstructured encounters in your daily life, like through hobbies, your children's school, or events, to more structured interactions like coaching and mentoring. In these interactions, it's crucial to be a keen listener, focusing on gaining perspectives from others rather than dominating the conversation. Asking questions and taking note of what surprises you during conversations allows for reflection and learning.

The network that has proven most invaluable to me is YPO, the Young Presidents' Organization. YPO is a global leadership community comprising over 29,000 chief executives from 130 countries, all committed to the idea that the world needs better leaders. These members have all achieved CEO status before the age of 45 and collectively lead businesses and organizations contributing USD 9 trillion in annual revenue. YPO's mission is to foster growth and improvement, both as leaders and as individuals, through peer learning and unique experiences within an inclusive and trust-based community.

When you join YPO, you'll hear a common refrain: "The more you put in, the more you get out." This principle holds true for both YPO and life in general. As someone who seeks to make the most of life, I've always been focused on accelerating my learning. I developed a personal learning model at an early age, recognizing the value of learning from peers, which is why YPO appealed to me. Having spent my entire career with one company, I craved different business perspectives. While learning by doing is potent, it also takes time. To expedite and enhance your learning, you should engage with and learn from others—externally driven learning.

One of YPO's signature features is the Forum. Forums consist of small groups of members who meet in an atmosphere of confidentiality, respect, and trust to learn from one another and exchange ideas. YPO pioneered the concept of Forum and provides the gold standard experience. Members can choose to participate in a chapter, network, or regional forum based on their interests. Forums meet monthly and host an annual member retreat. YPO also offers Forums for spouses/partners and young adult children. For me, the Forum experience is one of the most rewarding and valuable aspects of YPO.

A Forum is akin to a Personal Board where you gain diverse perspectives that you might not encounter elsewhere. All Forum members are business leaders who are peers with no conflicting interests. As a result, Forum members face similar challenges and engage in both personal and professional development. Forums follow a structured approach, and prospective members undergo training before joining. Confidentiality is paramount, and it's an unwavering belief that it will always be upheld. In my experience, all Forum members make the most of their time together, adhering to the high standards of the Forum.

My Personalized Learning Approach – Leadership in a Changing World

This section delves into the core principles of conscious leadership, emphasizing its timeless relevance while adapting to the dynamic landscape of transformative business. It explores how leaders can embody a conscious mindset, aligning with the Ubuntu Polder Framework's ethos to foster ethical practices, inclusivity, and sustainable decision-making. By intertwining timeless leadership values with adaptive strategies, this manifesto sets the stage for a new era of conscientious business leadership.

In a world marked by complex challenges rather than routine problems, leaders must be disruptors. They need to appreciate diverse perspectives, ask great questions, and frame challenges in ways that inspire innovative solutions. They should connect and build collaborative capacity within their organizations, encourage engagement, and understand what makes their organization unique. Survival hinges on adaptability and the ability to drive change.

I maintain a diverse reading regimen, exploring a variety of subjects in different languages. My team often comments on my reading speed, but in truth, I read at a normal pace. What sets me apart is my consistency—I read regularly as part of my winding-down routine before sleep. Interestingly, the only book I've started three times and have yet to finish is "speed reading," a testament to the value of savoring the reading experience.

Everyone has their unique pace and approach to learning. I've shared my method, but learning isn't an end in itself; it's a means to better comprehend the world, to envision more possibilities. In conjunction with our daily lives, learning brings us closer to wisdom—an embodied knowledge. Wisdom enables us to be effective leaders both at work and at home, benefiting not only our families and organizations but society as a whole.

The Power of Multisensory Learning: Understanding how we retain information is vital. Reading retains 20%, hearing retains 30%, seeing retains 40%, saying retains 50%, and doing retains 60%. However, combining visual, auditory, and verbal learning experiences achieves a remarkable 90% retention rate. This emphasizes the importance of going beyond reading and actively engaging with the world. Leaders must not only encourage learning but also motivate their teams to embrace it willingly, showing the value it holds for them.

The Role of Wisdom: Our world hungers for wisdom to navigate through challenges and make decisions that uplift communities, restore nature, and generate jobs. In the Ubuntu Polder Framework, learning, applying what we've learned, and learning from others are at its core. A conscious life, rich with experiences, whether through parenting, traveling, or tasting, keeps us in a perpetual learning mindset.

The Right Mindset: With the ever-evolving landscape of the 21st century, adopting the right mindset is crucial. It's a mindset that welcomes learning, unlearning, and relearning as not just a necessity but a profound opportunity for growth and, ultimately, for creating a brighter future.

Breaking Routines – Embrace Change and Embrace Life

David Bowie once wisely advised, "Never play to the gallery... Always remember that the reason that you initially started working is that there was something inside yourself that you felt that if you could manifest in some way, you would understand more about yourself and how you coexist with the rest of society. I think it's terribly dangerous for an artist to fulfill other people's expectations — they generally produce their worst work when they do that."

As we journey through life, we often look back and recognize the profound impact of seemingly small moments. Martin Lindstrom, a dear friend, acclaimed author, marketing guru, and *Time* magazine's Influential 100 Honoree, calls these moments "somatic markers." For me, one such somatic marker was an article I read about routines, written by a columnist I greatly admired, Renee Diekstra.

The Routine Dilemma: Diekstra's article shed light on the notion that routines, over time, can make us stop noticing the world around us. They accelerate the pace of life, pushing us into automatic mode. I yearned to live life to the fullest, akin to operating a camera in full manual mode, consciously choosing settings, focusing on what lies ahead, and directing my attention. I wanted to be able to change lenses, capture narrow or wide perspectives, and adapt to the ever-changing light. In essence, I sought to live life fully and consciously.

The Key to Full Consciousness: Breaking routines consistently became my compass for life. This philosophy inspired me to embark on a career as an expat, and I've never regretted it. As an expat, my family and I uproot ourselves every 3-5 years as we move from one country to another. While the discomfort of moving is undeniable, the experience of exploring the world is unparalleled. My driving force in life and my personal philosophy are intricately tied to this idea: Make breaking routines a habit to live life to the fullest.

Breaking Routines Beyond Travel: I've come to realize that breaking routines isn't limited to grand adventures but can be applied in more mundane aspects of life. Weight loss serves as a prime example. Concerns raised by my children about my health prompted me to change my routine. I shed 20 kilograms by altering my eating habits, maintaining a consistent sleep schedule, staying hydrated, and introducing regular physical activity. However, at one point, my body reached a comfortable equilibrium, and I had to break my newly formed eating routine to continue making progress.

The Yin and Yang of Life: The concept of Yin and Yang is prevalent in the East, and it reflects life's inherent duality—good and bad, two sides to every story, and the relativity of truth. Embracing this principle helps us stay calm and find common ground during heated debates. This duality applies to routines as well; there are good and bad routines, and change, no matter the context, demands conscious effort.

An Everyday Example: Even the most mundane routines, like shaving for men, can become automatic. Try to change the sequence the next time you shave, and you'll notice how unfamiliar and uncomfortable it feels. Routine change forces us to be present, to engage consciously with the task at hand.

A Reminder from a Broken Ligament: The need to break routines was driven home when I experienced a ligament injury in my pinky finger. The injury required six to eight weeks of immobilization for proper healing. Suddenly, everyday tasks became arduous, highlighting how much we rely on routines. It served as a poignant reminder of how uncomfortable it can be to break those familiar patterns.

The Power of Purposeful Habits: Not all habits are detrimental. The key is to cultivate habits that serve your growth. Among these, I recommend keeping the habit of breaking routines when life becomes a series of daily rituals. It's a reminder to embrace change, stay conscious, and embrace life's ever-evolving journey.

On Sleep

Embracing Change and the Power of Restful Sleep:

David Bowie's Wisdom: David Bowie imparts a valuable lesson on combating the enemy of creative work—complacency. He suggests venturing beyond your comfort zone, diving deeper into unfamiliar waters, and pushing your boundaries. It's precisely in that place where your feet can't quite touch the bottom that you're poised to do something truly exciting.

My Exception: Sleep as a Superpower: While there's an exception to every rule, in my case, it's sleeping. I've maintained a consistent sleep routine and have always needed my sleep. For a long time, I considered it a weakness, enviously eyeing those who could stay awake into the late hours. By 9-10pm, I'd start feeling drowsy and willingly succumb to sleep. However, in recent years, I've come to realize that my regular sleep pattern isn't a weakness—it's my superpower. Adequate sleep leaves me well-rested, maintaining high levels of concentration during the day's myriad meetings, a critical attribute for a CEO. The need to be consistently present and provide leadership in meetings necessitates a substantial attention span.

The Importance of Sleep for Health: A colleague and friend, Peter Noszek, a former tennis pro and exceedingly fit individual, suffered a heart attack before turning 50. He attributed it to a lack of sleep. His experience solidified my belief in guarding the healthy habit of regular sleep as a precious asset.

The Morning Routine: Beginning the day on the right note is crucial. While the "5am Club" book focuses on the exact time to rise, the key lesson is establishing a healthy morning routine. Engaging in meditation and exercise at the start of the day sets a positive tone. It helps boost your mood, engender a sense of accomplishment, and infuse your working day with energy. As a leader, your energy influences those around you, so fostering a culture of positive energy has been a priority in my teams.

My Morning Ritual: My personal morning routine involves several key elements. Upon waking, I prepare a protein shake infused with coffee, take a vitamin B pill, and concoct a blend of water with electrolytes and minerals, along with a squeeze of lemon, to consume during my workout. I then head upstairs to rouse my children, sometimes brewing them a cup of tea. Next, I embark on my exercise routine, whether it's a brisk walk, a light workout, or a session on my Kickr indoor bike. As I exercise, I listen to music or a podcast to get into the flow and reflect on the day's agenda and upcoming events.

Capturing Key Thoughts: During my exercise routine, I make sure to jot down high-level thoughts that cross my mind. These notes serve as a foundation to delve deeper into these ideas later. This practice allows me to revisit certain subjects over time, which reduces stress and aids comprehension. "Sleeping over it," as the saying goes, can be incredibly useful. This method extends to my work, study, and learning process. I revisit my notes regularly to ensure a thorough understanding of the subject, with several reviews spaced out over time. As an important speech, presentation, or exams approach, I create personal summaries and share notes with friends, who often provide unique perspectives and angles I might have missed.

Pen and Paper: Notably, I adhere to using pen and paper for this process, favoring it over typing on computers, laptops, or phones. This tactile approach facilitates better retention and comprehension.

On Intelligence

The Myriad Facets of Intelligence: Beyond IQ: In our society, it's intriguing how we've fixated on one facet of intelligence, namely IQ. However, I firmly believe that talent and intelligence, while important, can be overrated. Instead, I place my trust in discipline and unwavering hard work as the true keys to success. Our educational system predominantly emphasizes memorization and IQ, but in the realms of business and life, a holistic intelligence and consciousness are paramount.

My Early Awakening: I vividly recall encountering the groundbreaking book *Emotional Intelligence* by Daniel Goleman in 1995, during the transition from my educational journey to the professional world. This book immediately struck a chord with me. I wondered why our educational system hadn't incorporated empathy into its curriculum. Empathy is an essential trait for successful collaboration and task completion. Jack Ma, for instance, has his version of emotional intelligence, which he calls "LQ" or "love quotient." It underscores the significance of not only caring for your customers but also showing love and care for your team. This aspect is often underestimated, even though we all acknowledge that motivated individuals perform better when they feel a sense of belonging and genuine concern.

The Power of EQ and Its Subtopics: I was equally impressed by Shirzad Chamine's "Positive Intelligence" (PQ), which underscores the importance of emotional self-regulation. Recognizing negative emotions and steering towards a calm, positive, constructive, and creative state, referred to as "Sage mode," is crucial. LQ, PQ, and EQ are all interconnected, with LQ and PQ serving as deeper subtopics of emotional intelligence.

The Emergence of BQ: Another intriguing facet, "Body Quotient" or BQ, is gaining traction. It explores how our bodies continuously receive sensorial stimuli, which, upon interpretation, influence our emotions and, ultimately, our consciousness. Listening to your body, paying heed to gut feelings, or noticing physical responses to emotional stimuli plays a pivotal role in expanding situational awareness. The concept of "interoception" underscores the importance of incorporating your gut feelings into your decision-making process. This broader sense-making approach can be invaluable.

The Role of Soft Skills: In today's world, we tend to emphasize hard skills over soft skills, and I believe this is a fundamental issue in our society. Focusing excessively on hard skills in education, business, and society at large is, in my view, one of the root causes of our challenges and the impending crisis in consumer capitalism. This skewed emphasis places us on a collision course with reality.

The Essence of BQ in Jiu Jitsu: Jiu jitsu, a discipline that relies on using physics to conserve energy and triumph in combat, provides a clear example of why BQ should precede EQ and IQ. Children often grasp the fundamental principles of jiu jitsu intuitively because it aligns with their innate understanding of nature and the world's laws. However, as adults, we are often subjected to a method that breaks down techniques into memorizable steps, emphasizing IQ and EQ before BQ. With practice, we progress to a state where we can focus on the opponent's physical cues and respond instinctively, akin to being in the flow of BQ, EQ, and IQ.

Listening to Our Sensorial Nature: Humans are inherently social and sensorial beings. This aspect is poignantly depicted in movies like *Avatar*. It should be evident to us that we must tap into our inherent nature and not disregard what our bodies are telling us. The book on the gut as the "second brain" provides further insights into this connection.

The Power of Beliefs and Narratives: When faced with challenges, every leader must sift through facts and select the most pertinent data to construct a narrative that guides their decisions and actions. Therefore, selecting the right and relevant data is crucial in forming a representative reality, leading to informed assumptions and sound conclusions. It's essential to understand that the stories we tell ourselves shape our beliefs, which, in turn, steer our actions. We often consider our deep-seated beliefs as the ultimate truth, acting in alignment with them without regularly scrutinizing their validity.

Challenge Assumptions and Break Routines: The critical question we need to address is, "What don't I know that may be influencing my behavior?" This, in essence, is about continually challenging our assumptions and making it a habit to identify and disrupt routines.

Happiness

Every morning, I wake torn between a desire to save the world and an inclination to savor it. This makes it hard to plan the day. But if we forget to savor the world, what possible reason do we have for saving it? In a way, the savoring must come first. — *E.B. White*

Time is a river that sweeps me along, but I am the river; It is a tiger which destroys me, but I am the tiger; It is a fire which consumes me, but I am the fire. — *Jorge Luis Borges*

We need to learn how to want what we have, not to have what we want, in order to achieve steady and stable happiness. — *Tenzin Gyatso*

In a heartfelt letter to my son Louis, this section explores the profound connection between conscious leadership and happiness. It underscores the importance of fostering a workplace culture that prioritizes the well-being of individuals. Drawing on personal experiences and reflections, the letter captures the essence of how conscious leadership, as exemplified by the Ubuntu Polder Framework, contributes to the collective happiness of teams and stakeholders. It serves as a poignant reminder that ethical leadership goes hand in hand with creating environments where joy and fulfillment flourish.

Together, these sections articulate a compelling manifesto for conscious leadership within the Ubuntu Polder Framework. They provide actionable insights, personal anecdotes, and a vision for leaders to not only navigate the complexities of transformative business but also to lead with purpose, ethics, and a genuine commitment to the well-being of all involved.

Happiness can be cultivated and is critical to sustain the momentum of meaningful change. Statistics guru Hans Rosling, in his famous TED Talk, demonstrated how global development has objectively been nothing short of miraculous. We have made major progress in lifting people out of poverty, and yet many in our world are not happy. Despite living better than kings did not too long ago, they feel like they are falling behind and can barely make ends meet. Our society has educated us to always want more, to become richer, to buy more, and have more. The world needs to be re-educated. I've tried to impart a more balanced view of the world to my children, and, as I wrote to my eldest son Louis, scientists have studied happiness and have formulated a formula for it.

Enduring happiness: genes (44-50%) + circumstances & luck (25%) + portfolio of habits (25%)

It is true that much is given to us; we don't choose our genes and circumstances & luck at the start of life. Therefore, we should focus on what we can control—our habits: faith & life philosophy + family + community & friends + meaningful work (earned success and service to others). The global development advances that Hans talks about have improved the circumstances of most people and have allowed the genes of mankind to improve. But the portfolio of habits needs to be worked on by everyone individually.

Arthur Brooks, in his "Meaning and Happiness in Our New World," talks about avoiding unhealthy passions. Money, fame, prestige, power are unhealthy because they are never enough. The solution lies in the satisfaction equation S=Have/Want, as you must make sure H and W are in balance. The best way to do this is to manage your wants.

You can be happy and unhappy at the same time. Most people are conservative and aren't truly happy because they fear disappointment. Yet, no matter how hard, you should never postpone doing what you dream of to avoid fear; lean into it. Look at FEAR as False Evidence Appearing Real. So whenever you can, reframe and get new evidence and go for it. If something doesn't work out as expected, acknowledge, "I am disappointed," but not regretful. Recognize and be proud that you did nothing wrong. You tried, and if you can't change the outcome, resolve, 'I choose to accept the current circumstances and move forward.'

Other critical ingredients in cultivating happiness include being well-rested and practicing gratefulness. Therefore, force yourself to build enough recovery time for peak performance, just like athletes schedule recovery time. My recovery activities include playing golf, practicing photography, and scheduling small trips.

In terms of gratefulness, understand your "why" for feeling grateful. Then repeat it daily and build it into your routines. Throughout my career, I've reminded myself that I feel truly grateful for my health, my family, what I do, and the care I've been entrusted to grow my employees and the business.

Allow me to share how I've lived it. In the letter below, which I sent to my son a few years ago, I shared some life wisdom with him as he embarked on his student life abroad. But with you, I want to go beyond and share nuggets for use in business. I feel the need to start a dialogue with the next generation of leaders in this world, as the world today feels directionless and leaderless. We must have a debate on how to move forward and regain consciousness.

My dear son Louis,

Nowadays we are constantly overwhelmed with messages coming from all sides and it is important to sometimes slow down and get away from the non-stop noise.

I therefore send you some of my thoughts about life the old-fashioned way, a handwritten letter.

I want to start with what is most important; Papa loves you and will always be there for you!

You might not always feel being heard or understood by me and I apologize for that. I am trying my best, in my way, to guide you and to prepare you for life by passing on to you the learning from my own experiences, from how I handled what life has thrown at me, to allow you to avoid making my mistakes and become happier and more accomplished in your life!

I have also been a teenager and have also struggled with daunting questions like; what's the meaning of life, who am I, am I good enough, what is my purpose in this world?

Even though I try to pass-on my stories and values, you like me will make mistakes. Because making mistakes is human. When you do: stop, reflect on them, learn from it, and move on a bit wiser.

In this letter I want to again share some of my beliefs. To make it in any walk of life, we have to maintain good relations with others, based on trust. Therefore, be humble, don't be afraid to ask for forgiveness and be kind.

As life has a way of throwing many challenges at us, I have learnt the importance of managing your own life satisfaction levels and to be at ease that everything happens for a reason. We should not wait for golden opportunities, instead find gold in the opportunities, especially in learning from our mistakes.

Many scientists have studied happiness for many years, and they discovered the formula: 50% genes (uncontrollable) + 25% circumstances & luck (partially controllable) + 25% habits (fully controllable) = Happiness. The breakdown of habits: Faith + Family + Friends + Meaningful occupation. The meaningful occupation brings happiness through both the earned success from your efforts, but also the service and helping to others.

Now the good news is that you don't have to be like Papa or Mama, you just must be you.
But again, Papa and Mama will always be there to help you make sense of whatever you are struggling with.

Let me end by quoting from a book by Dr. Seuss that I used to read to you, Celina and Raphael when you were young:

Today you are YOU,
That is truer than true,
There is no one alive,
Who is Youer than YOU!

I love you,
Papa Bruno

My Ubuntu Polder Framework: A Journey Beyond Corporate Boundaries

The decision to transition from a thriving corporate career to establishing my consultancy and advisory firm, Ubuntu, in the vibrant landscape of the UAE was a pivotal moment in my Ubuntu Polder journey. After 27 years navigating the intricate corridors of corporate life, I realized the time had come to channel my passion for holistic business transformation into a venture that aligned with my vision for positive change.

Ubuntu, based in the heart of the Middle East, provides a strategic base for me to extend my reach across Asia, Africa, and Europe. The mission is clear: to collaborate with companies aspiring to make a tangible impact by embedding digital, sustainability, circularity, and ESG principles at the core of their business models. This shift from aspiration to reality requires more than loose projects; it demands a comprehensive, coordinated approach that translates into financial value.

The Catalyst for Change: The realization dawned that companies often embark on the journey towards holistic transformation but face challenges in execution, leading to failed attempts or scattered initiatives. My decision to establish Ubuntu was fueled by the desire to bridge this gap, turning aspirations into tangible, mutually beneficial outcomes. Through Ubuntu, I work closely with CEOs and leadership teams to ensure a WIN-WIN-WIN scenario, where impact-driven strategies not only benefit the company's bottom line but also uplift communities and preserve nature.

Leveraging Expertise and Networks: Drawing on my extensive experience across various companies and industries, I bring a wealth of knowledge in driving transformation across the entire end-to-end value stream. Ubuntu is not just a consultancy; it's a collaborative ecosystem, tapping into a vast network of experts to deliver a holistic approach that aligns with the principles outlined in this book.

Coordinated Holistic Approach: The Ubuntu Polder Framework is not just a theoretical concept; it's the guiding philosophy behind every engagement. I work hand-in-hand with leadership teams, ensuring a coordinated approach that maximizes the positive impact on all fronts. From digital integration to sustainability practices, circularity initiatives to ESG alignment, the journey is mapped out strategically, emphasizing interconnectedness and creating value at every step.

A Family Decision, a Rewarding Journey: Relocating with my family and embarking on this entrepreneurial venture was a monumental step, marked by both excitement and challenges. Starting from scratch in a new landscape is not without its complexities, but the vision of contributing to a sustainable, impactful business world propels the journey forward.

As Ubuntu takes root in the UAE, the journey unfolds as a testament to the belief that business can be a force for good. The Ubuntu Polder Framework is not just a framework; it's a way of life, and through Ubuntu, I am committed to shaping a future where companies thrive by creating value for themselves, their communities, and the environment.

Championing Conscious Leadership: Guiding the Next Wave of Positive Impact

At the heart of the Ubuntu Polder Framework lies a profound belief in conscious leadership—a leadership style that goes beyond the conventional and seeks to create a positive impact on the world. In the dynamic landscape of today's business environment, conscious leadership is not just an option; it is a necessity. As I embark on this transformative journey with Ubuntu, my commitment to fostering conscious leadership is unwavering, recognizing its pivotal role in shaping the new paradigm of doing business.

The need for Conscious Leadership in a world grappling with complex challenges, from environmental sustainability to social inequality, conscious leadership emerges as a beacon of hope. It involves leaders who are not just focused on profit margins but are deeply attuned to the interconnectedness of business, society, and the environment. The Ubuntu Polder Framework inherently incorporates the principles of conscious leadership, emphasizing cooperation, empathy, and a holistic approach to business transformation.

Mentoring the Next Generation beyond my role as an advisor and consultant, I am driven by a passion to nurture the leaders of tomorrow. Recognizing that the future lies in the hands of entrepreneurs and dynamic youth leaders, I am committed to mentoring them on their journey to creating a positive impact in society. Through mentorship, I aim to instill the values of conscious leadership, guiding them to navigate the complexities of the modern business landscape with a keen sense of purpose and responsibility.

Entrepreneurial Ventures with a Purpose: Mentoring extends beyond imparting knowledge; it involves actively supporting entrepreneurs in their ventures. Whether they are launching startups or leading dynamic projects, I am dedicated to ensuring that their initiatives align with the principles of the Ubuntu Polder Framework. It's about fostering a mindset where success is not solely measured by financial gains but by the positive contributions made to communities and the environment.

A Holistic Approach: Conscious leadership is not a standalone concept; it is intricately woven into the fabric of the Ubuntu Polder Framework. Through Ubuntu, I integrate conscious leadership principles into every advisory and consultancy project, creating a ripple effect that extends beyond the boardroom and into the wider world. The goal is to inspire leaders who not only drive organizational success but also contribute to the well-being of society and the preservation of our planet.

A Commitment to Positive Impact: As Ubuntu takes firm roots in the landscape of advisory and consultancy, the commitment to conscious leadership and mentorship remains steadfast. It's not just about transforming businesses; it's about nurturing a generation of leaders who recognize the transformative power they hold and wield it responsibly for the greater good. The Ubuntu Polder Framework, coupled with conscious leadership, becomes a catalyst for positive change, shaping a future where businesses thrive by creating value in harmony with society and nature.

Living Fully: A Poetic Reflection

In our journey towards holistic business transformation and the Ubuntu Polder Framework, it's crucial not only to focus on the evolution of businesses but also on the personal growth and fulfillment of individuals. The wisdom of renowned poets often captures the essence of life's profound truths. Let's reflect on a poem by Pablo Neruda, a Chilean poet whose words resonate with the spirit of embracing change and living a rich, purposeful life.

> *You start dying slowly;*
> *if you do not travel,*
> *if you do not read,*
> *If you do not listen to the sounds of life,*
> *If you do not appreciate yourself.*
> *You start dying slowly:*
> *When you kill your self-esteem,*
> *When you do not let others help you.*
> *You start dying slowly;*
> *If you become a slave of your habits,*
> *Walking everyday on the same paths...*
> *If you do not change your routine,*
> *If you do not wear different colours*
> *Or you do not speak to those you don't know.*

You start dying slowly:
If you avoid to feel passion
And their turbulent emotions.
Those which make your eyes glisten
And your heartbeat fast.
You start dying slowly:
If you do not risk what is safe for the uncertain
If you do not go after a dream
If you do not allow yourself
At least once in your lifetime
To run away from sensible advice
Don't let yourself die slowly
Do not forget to be happy!

SIX

CONCLUSION: EMBRACING THE UBUNTU POLDER FRAMEWORK FOR HOLISTIC IMPACT

BLUEPRINT FOR SUSTAINABLE SUCCESS IN THE DIGITAL AGE

want to express my deep gratitude for joining me on this enlightening journey through the Ubuntu Polder Framework, an approach that redefines the purpose of business and challenges us to embrace a more conscious, ethical, and sustainable approach to leadership and life. As we conclude this discourse, let us reflect on the key principles, the imperative need for change, and the invaluable takeaways from this new way of doing business, all underpinned by the advantages of conscious leadership, the embrace of digital technology, and the importance of understanding all business stakeholders.

Embracing Uncertainty and Change

In a world characterized by relentless uncertainty and rapid change, we must first recognize that embracing uncertainty is the key to progress. Change should not be feared; it should be embraced as an adventure filled with uncharted possibilities. In this dynamic landscape, it is not necessary to possess all the answers; instead, it is crucial to ask the right questions and listen to the environment and the tensions in the lives of our consumers.

The Power of Conscious Leadership

Conscious leadership stands as the cornerstone of the Ubuntu Polder Framework. Leaders of the new era are characterized by trust, empathy, active listening, and an unwavering commitment to the well-being of their teams. Trust, rooted in meritocracy, serves as the cornerstone of this leadership style, promoting productivity, inclusivity, and unity. Leadership is not about being in charge but about caring, recognizing individual talents, and fostering mutual support and loyalty within teams.

A Polder Framework for Business

The Ubuntu Polder Framework transcends the traditional business model, which has long prioritized profit above all else. It champions a holistic impact, where the "how" is as significant as the "what," and success is measured not only by financial gains but also by the ethical and sustainable integration of these principles into the business model. It redefines businesses as forces for good, emphasizing job creation and the restoration of nature, bringing value and purpose to society.

Embracing Digital Technology and AI

In this digital age, it is imperative for businesses to harness the power of technology, including artificial intelligence (AI). These tools offer unprecedented opportunities for innovation, efficiency, and understanding. AI can help businesses analyze vast amounts of data, predict trends, and make data-driven decisions that benefit not only the bottom line but also society at large. It is essential to leverage these technologies for the greater good, to solve complex problems, and to make businesses more sustainable and responsive to the needs of all stakeholders.

Understanding All Business Stakeholders and Forming Ecosystems

To truly transform business, it is essential to understand and engage with all stakeholders. Businesses do not exist in isolation; they are part of complex ecosystems that include customers, employees, suppliers, communities, and the environment. By comprehensively understanding these stakeholders, businesses can create ecosystems of collaboration and innovation to address societal issues. These ecosystems should be built on the principles of trust, transparency, and shared values. By working together, businesses can have a more significant and lasting impact, solving problems that transcend the boundaries of individual organizations.

Fostering a Common Platform and Narrative

Much like the dikes in the Netherlands, the world's old beliefs and institutions are under increasing pressure, and the lack of maintenance and updates has led to rising stress and anxiety on a global scale. A common platform and narrative are essential to drive a shift in these long-held beliefs and initiate necessary changes to address the world's impending challenges.

Incremental Change and Holistic Impact

Change need not be abrupt; it can be gradual, as long as it is directed towards the right path and taken with determination. We must not wait for magical solutions from external sources but should act within our spheres of influence to bring about positive change. Collaboration within ecosystems of like-minded individuals and organizations is essential. Intrinsic motivation and a commitment to being a force for good lead to both individual and collective happiness.

The Essence of Ubuntu – "I am because we are"

The African concept of Ubuntu emphasizes our interconnectedness and the idea that "I am because we are." This principle underscores the importance of unity and collaboration. We must remember that the essence of all businesses is to be a force for good, creating jobs and contributing to the restoration of nature, achieving holistic impact and integrating ethics and sustainability into the business model.

The Importance of Learning and Cultivating Consciousness

Learning is an ongoing journey, and the synergy of curiosity and passion compels us to experiment and grow. The pursuit of knowledge through formal education, reading, active listening, acquiring new skills, and self-reflection is vital. These principles of learning by doing foster leadership that is not solely driven by profit but also by the desire to improve society.

Shifting from Short-Termism to Problem-Solving

The current emphasis on quarterly results and short-termism, driven by Wall Street, is fundamentally unsustainable. We need to shift from a narrow pursuit of financial success to a broader focus on problem-solving. The Ubuntu Polder Framework challenges business schools to instill critical thinking and societal contribution, shifting the focus from wealth to the betterment of society.

The Three E's of Good Work – Excellence, Engagement, Ethics

The new breed of leaders should embody the three E's of Good Work: Excellence in their chosen fields, genuine Engagement with their work, and a strong sense of Ethics in their actions, shared with pride among family and friends.

Building Trust and Fostering Resilience

Trust is a measurable element of leadership, comprising credibility, reliability, and empathy, divided by self-orientation. Leaders should provide tools and support for self-improvement to team members and foster open and honest communication to build resilience, particularly in times of uncertainty.

The Power of Curiosity and Passion

Curiosity leads to a deep appreciation of the world's wonder and magic, while passion fuels the desire to engage fully in one's pursuits. The natural progression from curiosity and passion is experimentation, which brings knowledge, fostering infectious leadership that inspires others to achieve remarkable feats.

In conclusion, the Ubuntu Polder Framework, in the digital age and with a profound understanding of stakeholders and ecosystem-building, represents a transformative blueprint for businesses. It redefines business objectives, emphasizing ethical and sustainable practices, and nurturing conscious leaders who are committed to making a positive impact on society. As we navigate an ever-changing world, the Ubuntu Polder Framework and conscious leadership stand as guiding lights, illuminating the path towards a brighter, more sustainable future. Business becomes a force for good, making money and giving back, leaving an indelible mark on the world. The future is in our hands, and it is our collective responsibility to shape it for the better.

As business leaders, we stand at a crossroads of opportunity and responsibility. The Ubuntu Polder Framework beckons us to redefine success, not as a solitary pursuit, but as a collaborative journey toward shared prosperity. Let's shift our focus from finite gains to infinite impacts. Embrace Conscious Leadership, champion the interconnectedness of business, and embark on the Ubuntu Polder journey. It's a call to transform, not just our companies but the very fabric of how we do business. Are you ready to shape a legacy that echoes through generations? The time for conscious action is now. Let Ubuntu guide our decisions, amplify our impact, and together, let's build a future where business isn't just a force for good but a force for greatness. Thank you, and let's begin this transformative journey together and create Holistic Impact.

ABOUT THE AUTHOR

With a diverse international career spanning over three decades, Bruno has cultivated a profound expertise in holistic business transformation. Born and raised in the Netherlands, Bruno embarked on an educational journey in France, studying business before venturing into the corporate world across Southeast Asia, South Asia, Africa, and Switzerland. After a successful 27-year career in various senior leadership roles, Bruno founded Ubuntu, a consultancy based in Dubai, UAE, dedicated to guiding companies through holistic business transformation. Ubuntu emphasizes embedding digital, sustainability, circularity, and ESG at the heart of business models, reflecting Bruno's belief in the power of business as a force for good.

In addition to leading Ubuntu, Bruno is a public speaker and advocate for the Ubuntu Polder Framework, a pioneering approach that underscores cooperation and the interconnectedness of the world to create sustainable value. Bruno's transition from corporate leadership to entrepreneurship and advisory roles exemplifies a commitment to not only adapting to change but also driving it for the greater good.

Since January 2024, Bruno has also taken on the role of Vice President for Central Africa with Seaboard, further enriching his extensive international experience and continuing his impact on global business practices.

Bruno's journey is a beacon for current and aspiring leaders, demonstrating that with ambition, resilience, and a forward-thinking mindset, it's possible to reinvent oneself while contributing positively to society and the environment.

Profit with Purpose, Growth with Grace

Bridging the Gap Between Business Success and Global Well-being.

Welcome, **fellow Doers, Seekers of Meaning, and Lovers of Life** who carry the weight of concern for our world. We stand at the brink, facing **urgent challenges that demand our collective consciousness**. It's not too late for us to rise, **lead consciously, and become the architects of a world that generates jobs, uplifts communities, and restores nature**. Let the **Ubuntu Polder Framework** be your compass in the pursuit of a meaningful contribution.

> **"Bruno challenges us to lead with purpose, break free from conventional boundaries, and show courage in our complex and fast-moving world."**
>
> —Paul Polman, business leader, campaigner, and co-author of *Net Positive: How Courageous Companies Thrive by Giving More Than They Take*

> **"I can attest to the transformative impact of Bruno's approach. This book offers invaluable insights derived from real-world experiences, guiding leaders to navigate the complexities of business with purpose and drive."**
>
> —Nandu Nandkishore, former Global CEO Nestlé Nutrition, Mentor Capitalist, Adjunct Professor at the Indian School of Business, co-author of *The Dance of Disruption and Creation: Epochal Change and the Opportunity for Enterprise*

> **"Bruno's relentless dedication to holistic impact resonates deeply with my own commitment to circularity. This is a must-read for all doers striving to make a meaningful difference in the world."**
>
> —Professor Gunter Pauli, entrepreneur, economist, and author of numerous books, including the seminal work *The Blue Economy: 10 Years, 100 Innovations, 100 Million Jobs*

UBUNTU

FSC

ISBN 978-1-63777-588-2
90000
9 781637 775882

www.ingramcontent.com/pod-product-compliance
Lightning Source LLC
Chambersburg PA
CBHW030521210326
41597CB00013B/981